SCHOLASTIC

GRADE 2

Morning Jumpstarts: Math

100 Independent Practice Pages to Build Essential Skills

Marcia Miller & Martin Lee

New York · Toronto · London · Auckland · Sydney
Mexico City · New Delhi · Hong Kong · Buenos Aires

Teaching Resources

Cover design by Scott Davis
Interior design by Melinda Belter
Interior illustrations by Teresa Anderko, Melinda Belter, Maxie Chambliss, Rusty Fletcher, James Graham Hale, Anne Kennedy, Maggie Smith, and Sydney Wright; © 2013 by Scholastic Inc.

Image credit, page 90 © Veniamin Kraskov/Shutterstock

978-93-8631-308-9

Reprinted by Scholastic India Pvt. Ltd. Dec 2018

Introduction

In your busy classroom, you know how vital it is to energize children for the tasks of the day. That's why *Morning Jumpstarts: Math, Grade 2* is the perfect tool for you.

The activities in this book provide brief and focused individual practice on grade-level skills children are expected to master. Each Jumpstart is a two-page collection of five activities designed to review and reinforce a range of math skills and concepts children will build throughout the year. The consistent format helps children work independently and with confidence. Each Jumpstart includes these features:

- Number Place
- Fast Math
- Think Tank
- Data Place
- Puzzler

You can use a Jumpstart in its entirety or, because each feature is self-contained, assign sections at different times of the day or to different groups of learners. The Jumpstart activities will familiarize children with the kinds of challenges they will encounter on standardized tests, and provide a review of skills they need to master. (See page 6 for a close-up look at the features in each Jumpstart.)

The Common Core State Standards (CCSS) for Mathematics serve as the backbone of the activities in this book. On pages 7–8, you'll find a correlation chart that details how the 50 Jumpstarts dovetail with the widely accepted set of guidelines for preparing children to succeed in math.

Generally, we have kept in mind the eight CCSS "mathematical practices" that should inform solid math exploration, calculation, and interpretation, even for the youngest learners.

Mathematical Practices

1. Make sense of problems and persevere in solving them.
2. Reason abstractly and quantitatively.
3. Construct viable arguments and critique the reasoning of others.
4. Model with mathematics.
5. Use appropriate tools strategically.
6. Attend to precision.
7. Look for and make use of structure.
8. Look for and express regularity in repeated reasoning.

A Look Inside

Each two-page Jumpstart includes the following skill-building features.

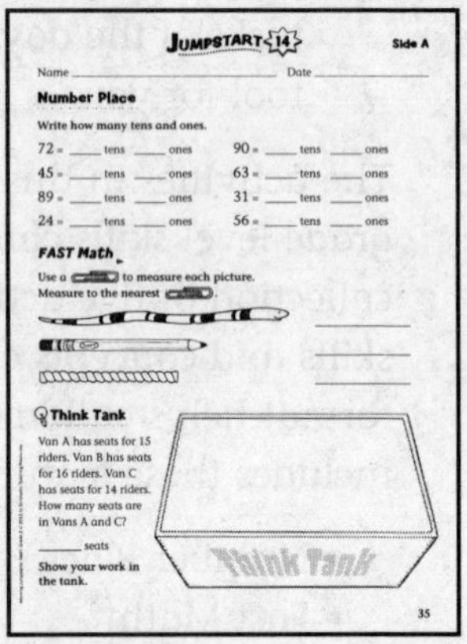

Number Place The first feature on Side A reviews grade-appropriate place-value skills related to whole numbers, counting, and groupings in tens and ones. Regardless of the particular presentation, children will use their knowledge of place value and their number sense to complete this feature. A solid place-value foundation is essential for success with computation and estimation, and for an overall grasp of numerical patterns and relationships.

Fast Math The second Side A feature addresses necessary grade-level computation skills with the goal of building automaticity, fluency, and accuracy. To work through these exercises, children draw upon their understanding of computation strategies and mathematical properties. In some instances, children will review skills that have been covered previously. This is a good way to keep math skills sharp and to point out to you where revisiting a skill or algorithm may be beneficial.

Think Tank This feature rounds out Side A by offering an original word problem that draws from a wide spectrum of grade-appropriate skills, strategies, and approaches. Some are single-step problems; others require multiple steps to solve. The think tank itself provides a place where children can draw, do computations, and work out their thinking. This is a particularly good section to discuss together, to share solutions, as well as to compare and contrast approaches and strategies. Encourage children to recognize that many problems can be solved in more than one way, or may have more than one solution.

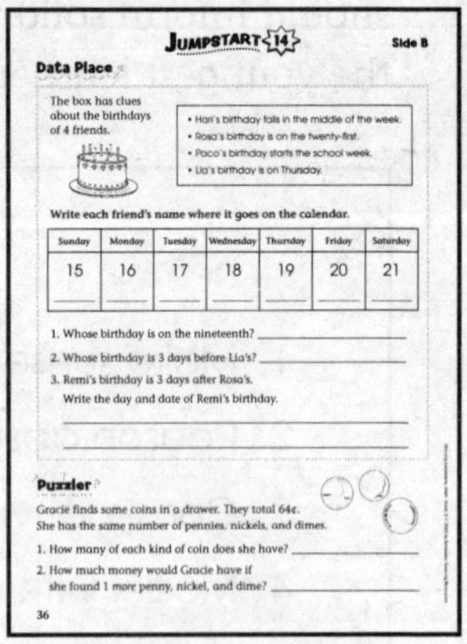

Data Place Every Side B begins with an activity in which children solve problems based on reading, collecting, representing, and interpreting data that is presented in many formats: lists, tables, charts, pictures, and, mostly, in a variety of graphs. In our modern, rapidly changing world, it is essential that children build visual literacy by becoming familiar with many kinds of graphic presentations. This feature presents the kinds of graphs children are likely to encounter online, on TV, and in newspapers and magazines. Many include data from other curriculum areas.

Puzzler Side B always ends with some form of an entertaining challenge: a brainteaser, puzzle, non-routine problem, code, or other engaging task designed to stretch the mind. While some children may find this section particularly challenging, others will relish teasing out trick solutions. This feature provides another chance for group work or discussion. It may prove useful to invite pairs of children to tackle these exercises together. And, when appropriate, invite children to create their own challenges, using ideas sparked by these exercises. Feel free to create your own variations of any brainteasers your class enjoys.

Name ______________________ Date ______________

Number Place

Write each number.

eight	
five	
nine	
seven	

three	
four	
one	
six	

ten	
two	

FAST Math

Add. Circle any answer that is your age.

4 + 2 = ______	3 + 2 = ______	1 + 7 = ______
3 + 4 = ______	5 + 1 = ______	2 + 6 = ______
6 + 3 = ______	7 + 2 = ______	5 + 5 = ______

Think Tank

Dan is 6 years old. Ella is 2 years older than Dan. Max is twice as old as Ella. How old is Max?

Max is ________ years old.

Show your work in the tank.

Data Place

**Count how many of each kind of button.
Tally them in the table.**

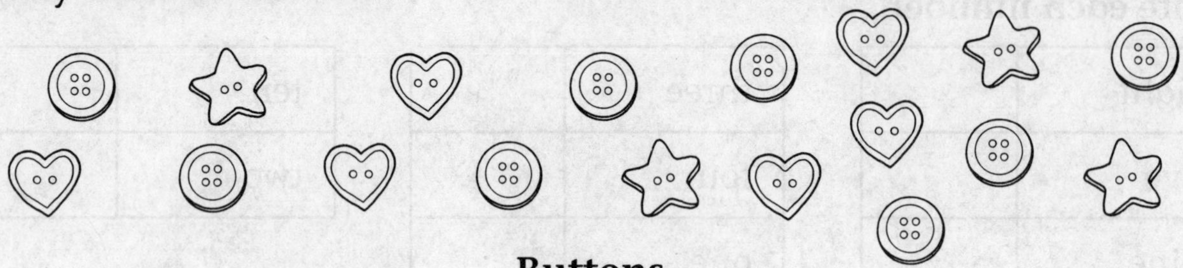

Buttons

Shape	Tallies

1. How many round buttons? _________

2. How many heart AND star buttons? _________

Puzzler

**Connect the dots in order.
Start at 1.**

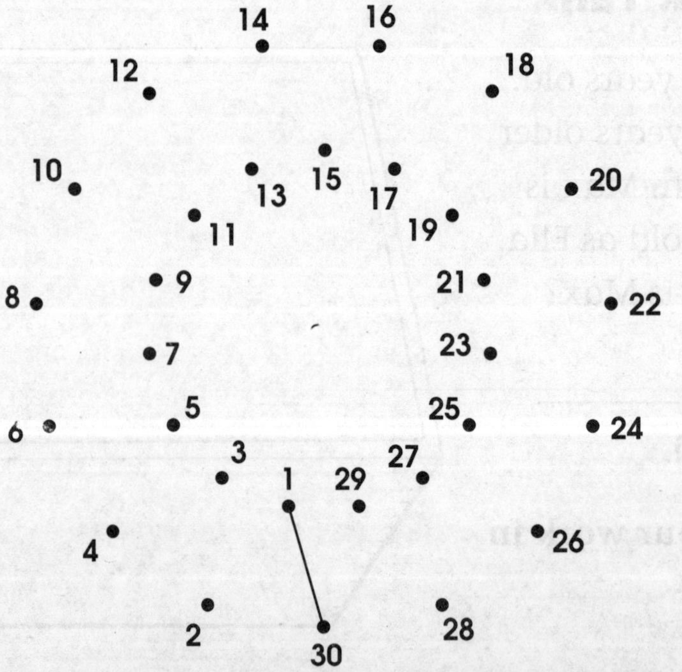

Name ____________________ Date ____________

Number Place

Draw lines to match words to numbers.

eleven	17	fourteen	19
fifteen	20	eighteen	16
twenty	13	sixteen	14
seventeen	15	nineteen	12
thirteen	11	twelve	18

FAST Math

Add. Circle any answer that is 19.

4 + 7 = ______	8 + 8 = ______	9 + 7 = ______
10 + 9 = ______	5 + 7 = ______	7 + 6 = ______
8 + 9 = ______	7 + 7 = ______	5 + 8 = ______

Think Tank

Read the science fact in the box. What is the fifteenth word?

____

Which word is fifth from the end?

____

The sun is a huge star.
It spins around in space far,
far from Earth. The sun is made
mostly of very hot gas.

Think Tank

JUMPSTART 2

Side B

Data Place

Use the picture graph to answer questions about Lee's fish.

Lee's Fish

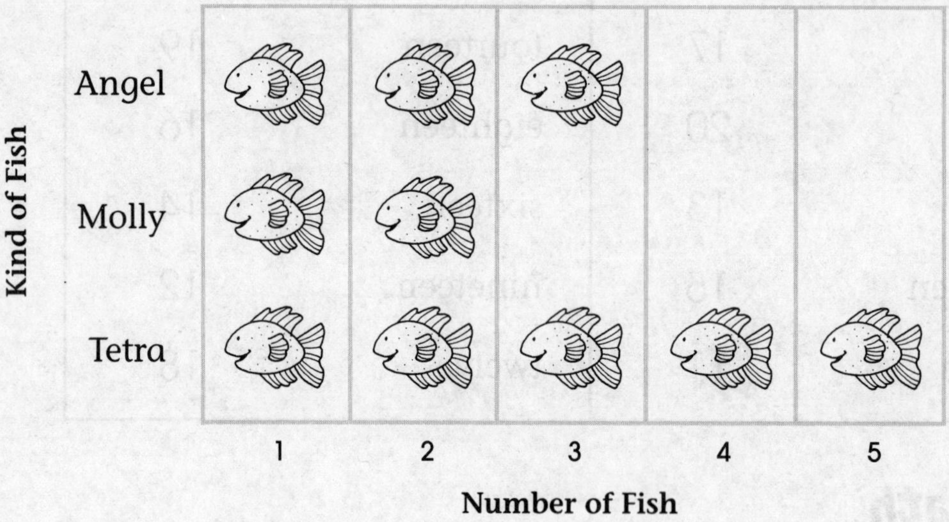

1. How many different kinds of fish does Lee have? ________

2. Lee has ________ angel fish.

3. Lee has 2 ____________________________ fish.

4. Lee has ________ more tetra fish than angel fish.

Puzzler

Write 1, 2, 3, 4, and 5 *once* in each empty box. Make each row ↔ and column ↕ have the SAME sum.

What is the sum in each row and column? ________

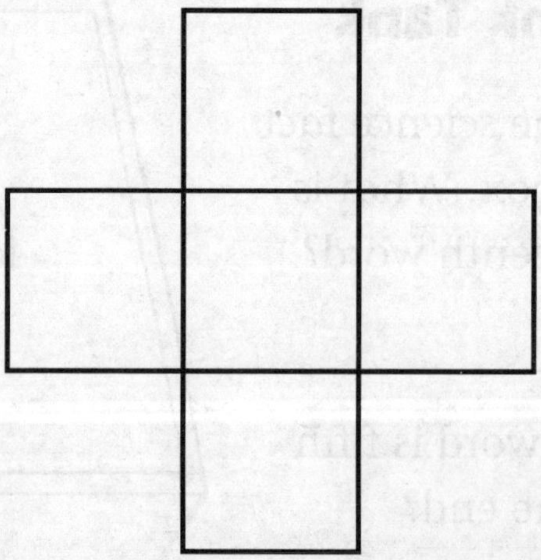

JUMPSTART 3

Side A

Name ______________________________ Date ______________

Number Place

Write all the missing numbers.

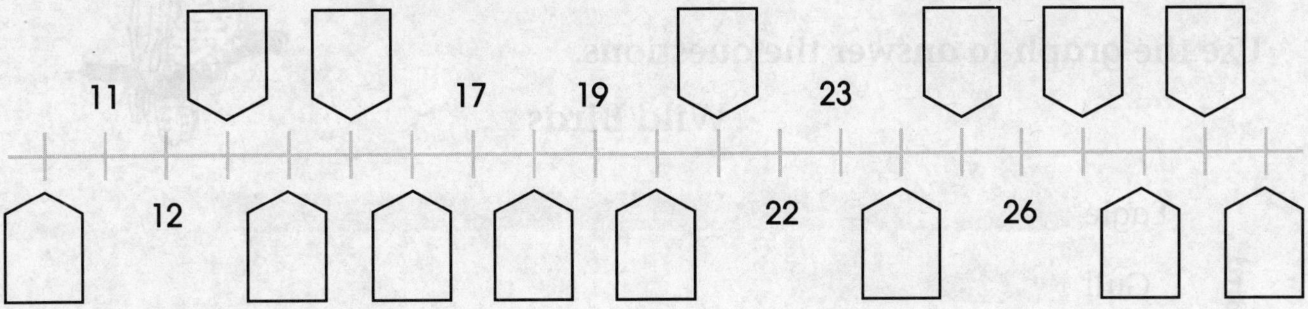

FAST Math

Add doubles.

4	8	6	9	5	7
+ 4	+ 8	+ 6	+ 9	+ 5	+ 7
___	___	___	___	___	___

Now write the sums in order from *least* to *greatest*.

____

Think Tank

A baker starts work at 6:00 A.M. He ends work at 3:00 P.M. How many hours does the baker work?

He works

______ hours.

Show your work in the tank.

Data Place

Mara's class learned about wild birds that live near the school. The children picked the bird they like best. Mara made a graph to show the votes.

Use the graph to answer the questions.

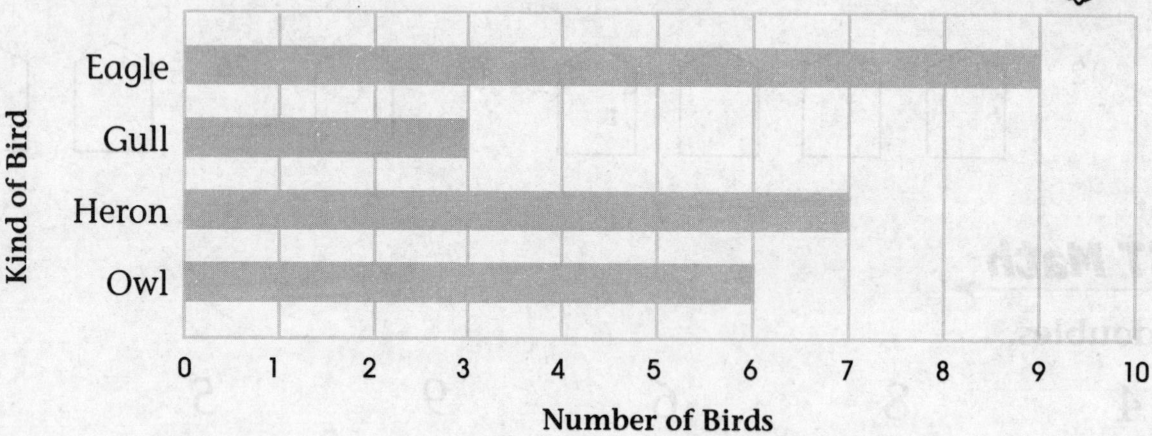

1. Which bird got the most votes? ________________

2. How many children voted for that bird? ________________

3. Which bird got 6 votes? ________________

Puzzler

Use *only* the shapes in the box below to make a picture. Turn the shapes or change sizes if you need to. Use every shape at least 3 times. Give the picture a title.

____

Name ____________________ Date ____________

Number Place

Color the third and sixth hats **yellow.**

Color the fourth and ninth hats **blue.**

Color the first and tenth hats **green.**

Color the second and eighth hats **red.**

Leave the fifth and seventh hats **white.**

FAST Math

Add. Circle the greatest sum.

3 + 7 + 4 = _____	5 + 2 + 6 = _____	8 + 3 + 5 = _____
6 + 1 + 8 = _____	9 + 6 + 4 = _____	5 + 9 + 4 = _____

Think Tank

I am a 2-digit even number. I am less than 60. Add my digits to get 12. Subtract one of my digits from the other to get 4. What number am I?

____

Show your work in the tank.

Data Place

Use the graph to answer the questions about people's favorite shapes.

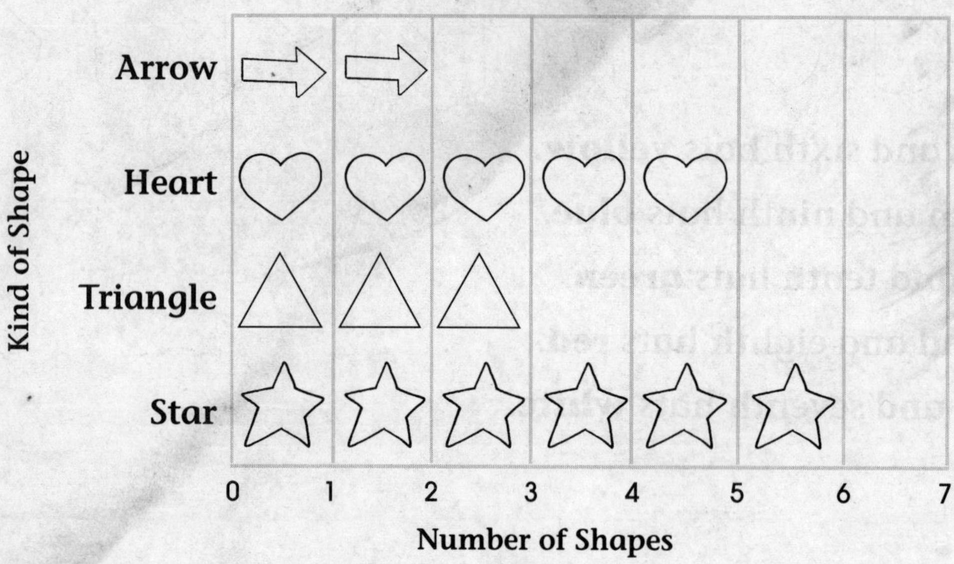

1. How many shapes are named in the graph? ________

2. Which shape got 5 votes? ________________

Puzzler

Add or subtract.
Use the key.

1.  +  = ________

2.  +  = ________

3.  +  = ________

4.  −  = ________

5.  −  = ________

6.  −  = ________

JUMPSTART 5

Side A

Name ______________________ Date ______________

Number Place

Write 11 to 20 below the eggs.

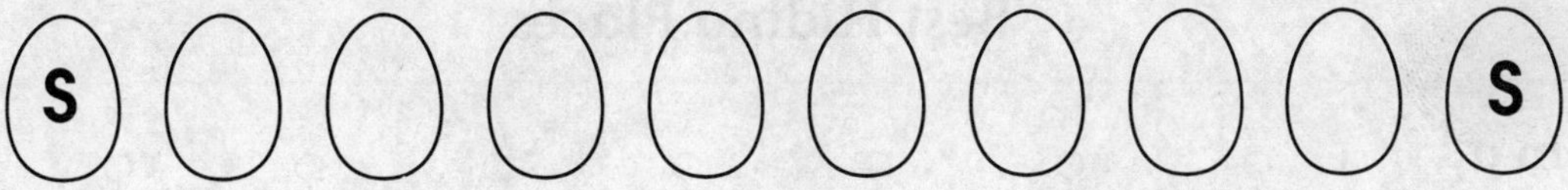

___ ___ ___ ___ ___ ___ ___ ___ ___ ___

Then write:

A in the fourteenth egg
B in the sixteenth egg
C in the twelfth egg
E in the eighteenth egg
L in the seventeenth egg
M in the fifteenth egg
R in the nineteenth egg and the thirteenth egg

What word did you spell? ______________________

FAST Math

Subtract. Circle all *even* answers.

10 – 2 = ______	8 – 6 = ______	7 – 1 = ______
9 – 7 = ______	6 – 5 = ______	10 – 3 = ______
8 – 5 = ______	7 – 4 = ______	9 – 5 = ______

Think Tank

Nell is fourth in a line of 9 kids. Aya is last in line. How many kids are between Nell and Aya?

______

Show your work in the tank.

Data Place

Use the graph about places people like to hide to answer the questions.

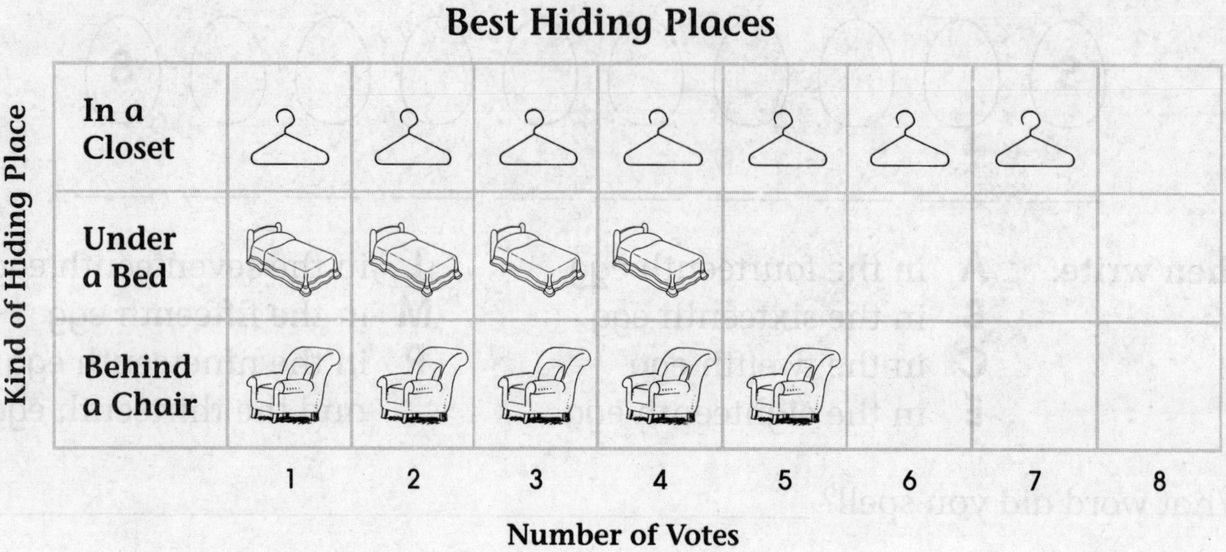

1. Where would 7 people hide? ____________

2. How many people would hide behind a chair? ____________

3. Order the 3 hiding places from *most* to *least* favorite.

____

Puzzler

Arrange 11 toothpicks to form a figure that looks like the word NINE. Draw a picture

Write how you solved the puzzle. ____________________

____

____

JUMPSTART 6

Side A

Name ______________________ Date ______________

Number Place

Write the number that comes just *after*.

36, ______	48, ______
77, ______	80, ______
53, ______	99, ______

FAST Math

Subtract. Circle all *odd* answers.

13 – 7 = ______	18 – 10 = ______	14 – 6 = ______
19 – 9 = ______	16 – 7 = ______	17 – 8 = ______
11 – 5 = ______	15 – 8 = ______	12 – 7 = ______

Think Tank

Tai invited 10 adults and 9 children to his party. But 2 adults and 3 children could not go. How many adults and how many children were at the party?

____

Show your work in the tank.

Data Place

Use the graph about rainy days to answer the questions.

Rainy Days

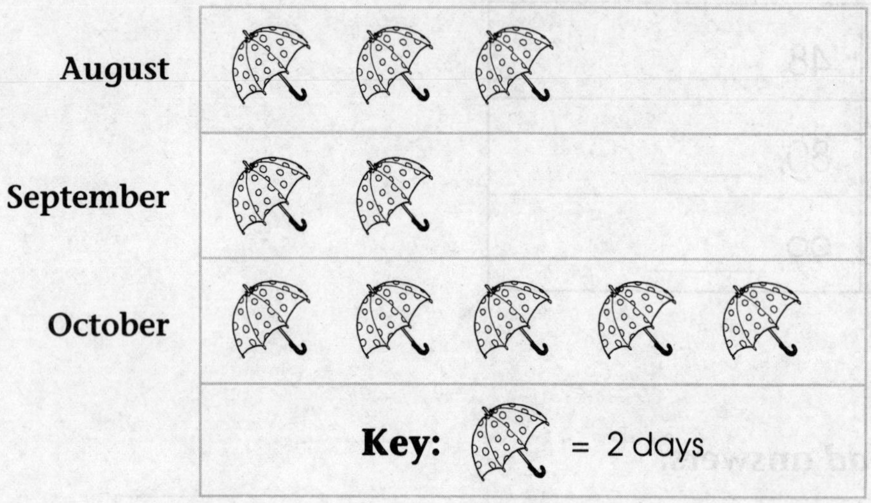

1. Which month was the rainiest? ______________

2. What does 1 umbrella mean? ______________

3. How many rainy days were there in August? ______________

Puzzler

Trace over every line in the house. But *don't* lift your pencil or go over the same line twice.

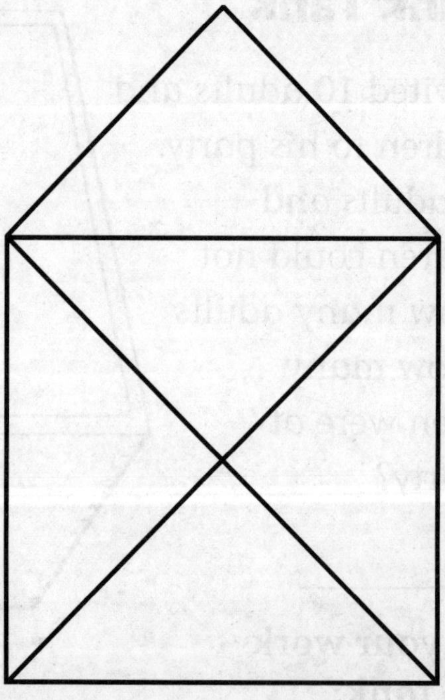

Hints:

- Try with your finger first.
- Start at a bottom corner.

JUMPSTART 7

Side A

Name ______________________ Date ______________

Number Place

Write the number that comes just *before*.

______, 74	______, 39	______, 90
______, 58	______, 67	______, 46

FAST Math

Subtract. Think about doubles.

$$\begin{array}{r} 18 \\ -\ 9 \\ \hline \end{array} \quad \begin{array}{r} 12 \\ -\ 6 \\ \hline \end{array} \quad \begin{array}{r} 16 \\ -\ 8 \\ \hline \end{array} \quad \begin{array}{r} 10 \\ -\ 5 \\ \hline \end{array} \quad \begin{array}{r} 14 \\ -\ 7 \\ \hline \end{array} \quad \begin{array}{r} 20 \\ -\ 10 \\ \hline \end{array}$$

______ ______ ______ ______ ______ ______

Now write the differences in order from *greatest* to *least*.

____

Think Tank

Ruben had 13 dollars.
He spent 5 dollars on
a movie ticket and
2 dollars on popcorn.
How much money
did he have left?

________ dollars

Show your work in the tank.

JUMPSTART 7

Side B

Data Place

Finish the table about cousins. Then answer the questions.

How Many Cousins?

Cousins	Tallies	Number
None	卌 |	
1 or 2	卌 ||	
3 or 4	卌 ||||	
5 or 6	卌	
7 or 8	||||	
9 or more	||	

How many people have:

1. no cousins? ______
2. 3 or 4 cousins? ______
3. 9 or more cousins? ______
4. How many cousins do 4 people have? ______

Puzzler

What is the tallest *and* heaviest bird in the world?

Use the clues below to solve the riddle.

______ ______ ______ ______ ______ ______ ______

The seventh letter is *h*.

The fifth letter is *i*.

The third letter is *t*.

The second letter is *s*.

The sixth letters is *c*.

The fourth letter is *r*.

The first letter is *o*.

Name ______________________ Date ______________

Number Place

Write the number that comes *between*.

38, ______ , 40	27, ______ , 29	342, ______ , 344
63, ______ , 65	56, ______ , 58	508, ______ , 510
49, ______ , 51	199, ______ , 201	775, ______ , 777

FAST Math

Add or subtract.
Circle the answer that is an *even* number.

$$\begin{array}{r}7\\+\ 4\\\hline\end{array}\qquad\begin{array}{r}9\\-\ 6\\\hline\end{array}\qquad\begin{array}{r}8\\+\ 9\\\hline\end{array}\qquad\begin{array}{r}12\\-\ 7\\\hline\end{array}\qquad\begin{array}{r}5\\+\ 8\\\hline\end{array}\qquad\begin{array}{r}13\\-\ 9\\\hline\end{array}$$

Think Tank

Linn has a rope 5 feet long. Kenya has a rope 7 feet long. The girls lay the ropes end-to-end. What is the total length?

____

Show your work in the tank.

Data Place

Roy sets the table for lunch. Count how many of each item he uses.

Make a pictograph. Use X for each item.

Item	How Many
Forks	
Glasses	
Knives	
Plates	
Spoons	
Key: X = 1 item	

Puzzler

Study the drawing. Find the sum of numbers:

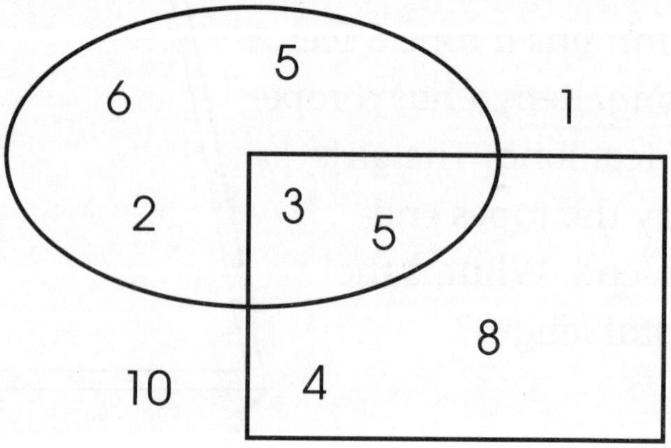

1. inside the oval AND box. ________
2. inside the oval ONLY. ________
3. inside the box ONLY. ________
4. outside both shapes. ________

JUMPSTART 9

Side A

Name ______________________ Date ______________

Number Place

Skip count aloud by 5s. Write each number you say.

5, 10, ____, ____, ____, ____, ____, ____, ____, ____,

____, ____, ____, ____, ____, ____, ____, ____, 100

FAST Math

Write each fact family.

8, 5, 13	9, 6, 15
____ + ____ = ____	____ + ____ = ____
____ + ____ = ____	____ + ____ = ____
____ − ____ = ____	____ − ____ = ____
____ − ____ = ____	____ − ____ = ____

Think Tank

Draw what comes next in each pattern.

✖ ● ✖ ● ✖ ● ✖ ____ ____ ____ ____

♥ = ☾ ♥ = ☾ ♥ ____ ____ ____ ____

◇ ▲ ◇ ▲ ◇ ▲ ◇ ▲ ◇ ____ ____ ____ ____

Think Tank

Data Place

Use the table to answer the questions.

Abe's Acorns

Day	Monday	Tuesday	Wednesday	Thursday	Friday
Acorns Found	37	27	18	29	15

1. How many acorns did Abe find on Tuesday? ____________
2. What happened on Friday? ____________
3. On which day did Abe find 18 acorns? ____________
4. On which day did Abe find almost 30 acorns? ____________
5. Which was Abe's best day for acorns? ____________

Puzzler

Unscramble the number words. Use the word bank to check your spelling.

Word Bank

zero	one	two	three	four
five	six	seven	eight	nine

ixs ____________

wot ____________

noe ____________

enin ____________

ozre ____________

ruof ____________

evif ____________

vesen ____________

ehert ____________

thige ____________

Name ____________________ Date __________

Number Place

Write each number.

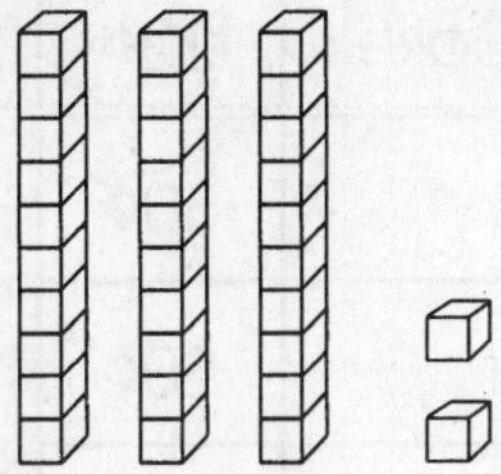

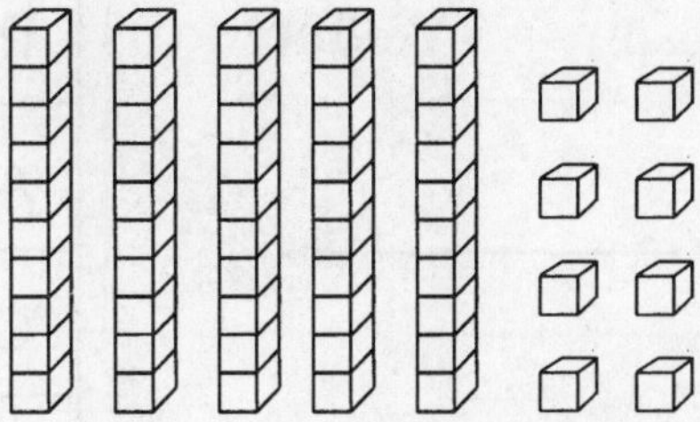

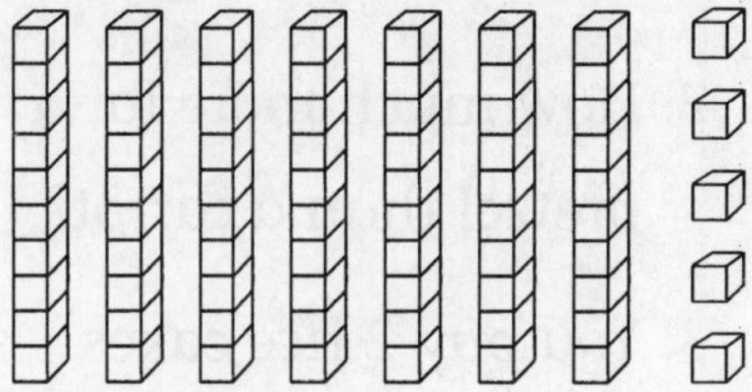

FAST Math

Add 40 to each number.	Subtract 30 from each number.
24 → ______	98 → ______
53 → ______	67 → ______
47 → ______	84 → ______

Think Tank

Dev buys a pen for $2, a cap for $4, and a book for $5. How much money does he spend in all?
Dev spends

______________ .

Show your work in the tank.

Data Place

Use the price list for Snow's Snack Shop to answer the questions.

Snow's Snack Shop

Snack	Price
Rice Cake	22¢
Apple	30¢
Carrot	20¢
Peanuts	25¢
Pretzel	35¢

1. Which snack costs 25¢? ________
2. How much more for a pretzel than a carrot? ________
3. You buy 2 rice cakes. How much do you spend? ________
4. You buy 3 carrots. How much do you spend? ________
5. You buy peanuts and 2 apples. How much do you spend? ________

6. You have 2 quarters. What would you buy? ________
7. How much would you have left? ________

Puzzler

Figure out each code.

1.  +  = 10, so  = ______
2.  +  = 18, so  = ______
3. So,  +  = ______
4. And  –  = ______
5.  +  = 20, so 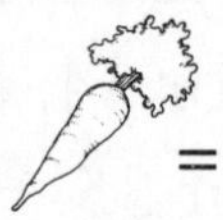 = ______
6.  +  = 14, so  = ______
7. So,  + 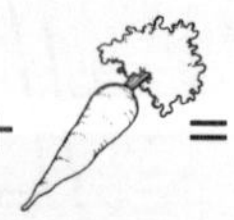 = ______
8. And  –  = ______

JUMPSTART 11

Side A

Name ______________________ Date ______________

Number Place

Write the number on the line.

tens	ones
4	5

______

tens	ones
3	1

______

tens	ones
2	8

______

tens	ones
6	7

______

tens	ones
7	9

______

tens	ones
5	0

______

FAST Math

Add or subtract. Circle the greatest answer.

$80 - 30 =$ ______

$40 + 50 =$ ______

$80 + 90 =$ ______

$140 - 70 =$ ______

$130 - 50 =$ ______

$70 + 60 =$ ______

Think Tank

Eva found 25¢ under the sofa. Then her dad gave her 3 nickels and 1 dime. How much money does Eva have now?

______

Show your work in the tank.

JUMPSTART 11

Side B

Data Place

Count the chairs, children, and windows in your classroom. Keep track of how many in the table.

Item	Tally	Number
Chairs		
Children		
Windows		

1. What was hard about this task? ______________________________

____

2. Why might kids get different results? ___________________________

____

Puzzler

Write the number for each clue.

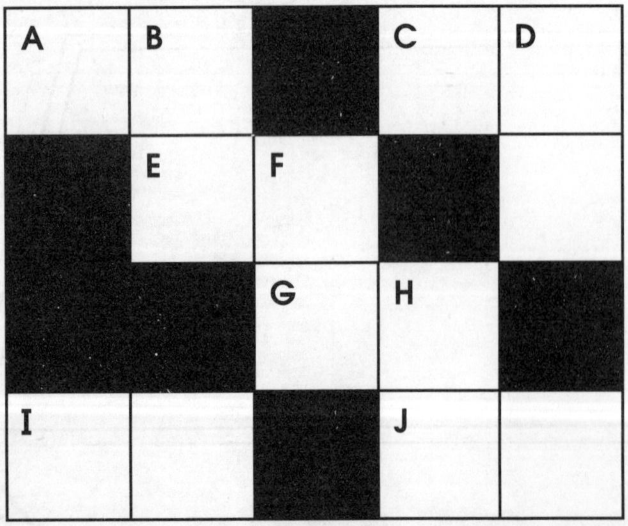

Across

A. forty-four

C. 20 + 3

E. 30 – 1

G. sixty-seven

I. 7 + 9

J. 8 tens + 3 ones

Down

B. 40 + 2

D. 40 – 2

F. ninety-six

H. seventy-eight

JUMPSTART 12

Side A

Name ____________________ Date ____________

Number Place

Write in number form.

thirty ____________ forty-one ____________

fifty-three ____________ eighteen ____________

ninety-nine ____________ thirty-six ____________

FAST Math

Write each time with A.M. or P.M.

Think Tank

Bryn is taller than Tia. Tia is taller than Felix. Felix is not taller than Jenna. Jenna is taller than Bryn and Tia. Who is the shortest?

____

Show your work in the tank.

JUMPSTART 12

Side B

Data Place

Use the table about loose teeth to answer the questions.

Child	How Many Loose Teeth?
Brian	1
Elvis	0
Kenny	2
Nina	1
Polly	2
Roberto	3
Tess	2
Wendy	1

1. Who has the most loose teeth? ____________________

2. Who has no loose teeth? ____________________

3. How many loose teeth does Kenny have? ________

4. Which children have 1 loose tooth? ____________________

Puzzler

Use the code to figure out each secret word.

A = 1	B = 2	C = 3	D = 4	E = 5	F = 6	G = 7
H = 8	I = 9	J = 10	K = 11	L = 12	M = 13	N = 14
O = 15	P = 16	Q = 17	R = 18	S = 19	T = 20	U = 21

8 15 20 ____________

18 9 4 5 ____________

10 1 13 ____________

17 21 9 20 ____________

16 5 14 ____________

3 8 5 19 19 ____________

JUMPSTART 13

Side A

Name ______________________ Date ____________

Number Place

Write in standard form.

3 tens 5 ones 35

8 tens 1 one ______

2 tens 6 ones ______

9 tens 3 ones ______

5 tens 7 ones ______

6 tens 0 ones ______

7 tens 8 ones ______

4 tens 2 ones ______

FAST Math

Draw hands to show each time.

quarter to 3

half past 10

30 minutes after 5

Think Tank

Lola picks 3 baskets of limes. One basket has 25 limes. Another basket has 22 limes. The third basket has 20 limes. How many limes has Lola picked in all?

____

Show your work in the tank.

Data Place

This is how Mr. Hay's students got to school today.

- Six took the bus.
- Five walked.
- Three rode bikes.
- Four came in cars.

Graph the data.

How Students Got to School

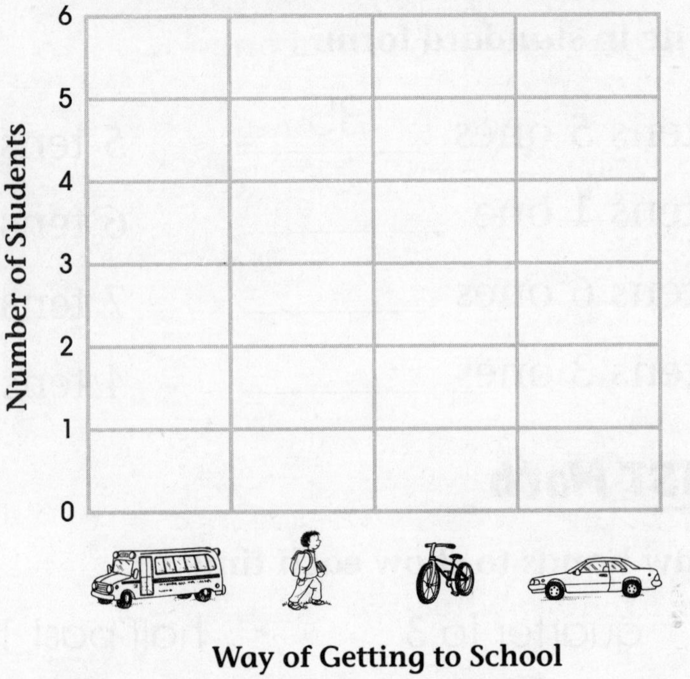

1. How many students got to school today? ____________
2. How many more walked than came in cars? ____________
3. Which way did the most students get to school? ____________________

Puzzler

Count by 2s to connect the dots.

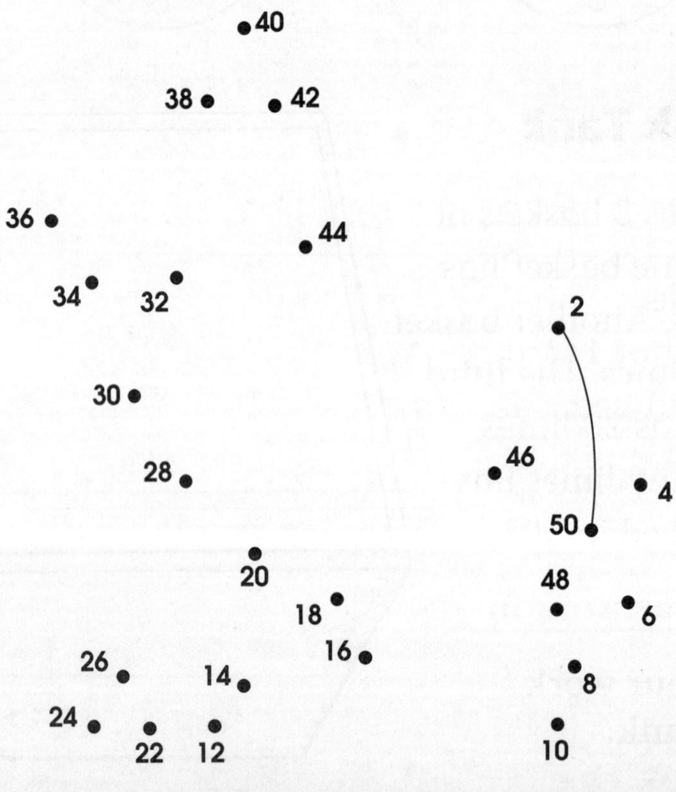

JUMPSTART 14

Side A

Name ______________________ Date ______________

Number Place

Write how many tens and ones.

72 = _____ tens _____ ones   90 = _____ tens _____ ones

45 = _____ tens _____ ones   63 = _____ tens _____ ones

89 = _____ tens _____ ones   31 = _____ tens _____ ones

24 = _____ tens _____ ones   56 = _____ tens _____ ones

FAST Math

Use a  to measure each picture.
Measure to the nearest .

____

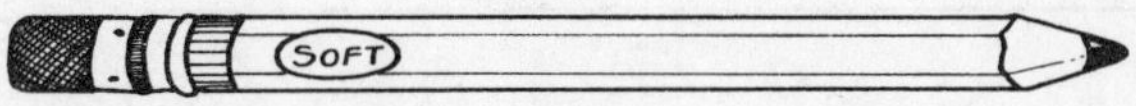

____

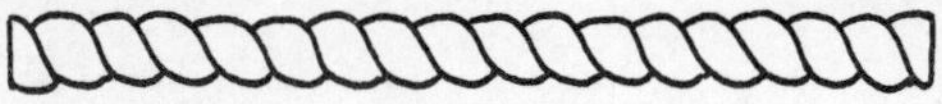

____

Think Tank

Van A has seats for 15 riders. Van B has seats for 16 riders. Van C has seats for 14 riders. How many seats are in Vans A and C?

_______ seats

Show your work in the tank.

Data Place

The box has clues about the birthdays of 4 friends.

- Hari's birthday falls in the middle of the week.
- Rosa's birthday is on the twenty-first.
- Paco's birthday starts the school week.
- Lia's birthday is on Thursday.

Write each friend's name where it goes on the calendar.

Sunday	Monday	Tuesday	Wednesday	Thursday	Friday	Saturday
15	16	17	18	19	20	21
______	______	______	______	______	______	______

1. Whose birthday is on the nineteenth? ________________
2. Whose birthday is 3 days before Lia's? ________________
3. Remi's birthday is 3 days after Rosa's.
   Write the day and date of Remi's birthday.
   ____
   ____

Puzzler

Gracie finds some coins in a drawer. They total 64¢.
She has the same number of pennies, nickels, and dimes.

1. How many of each kind of coin does she have? ________________
2. How much money would Gracie have if she found 1 *more* penny, nickel, and dime? ________________

JUMPSTART 15

Side A

Name ______________________ Date ______________

Number Place

Write in expanded form.

83 ___80 + 3___

56 ______________________

47 ______________________

35 ______________________

60 ______________________

FAST Math

Add or subtract.

14 feet	57 feet	42 inches	30 inches
+ 23 feet	– 35 feet	+ 27 inches	– 10 inches
________	________	________	________

Think Tank

I am a 3-digit number. The sum of my digits is 1. What number am I?

____

Show your work in the tank.

JUMPSTART 15

Side B

Data Place

Make the same money amount in different ways.
Use the chart to show some ways to make **57¢**.

				Total
2	0		2	57¢
2	0	0		57¢
1	0	6		57¢
1		2		57¢
0				57¢
0				57¢

Puzzler

Solve the number puzzle.
Fill each small square with 1, 2, 3, or 4.
Use each number *once* in every row ⟷ and *once* in every column ↕.

	4	2	
1	2		4
		4	3
4	3		

Name ______________________ Date ____________

Number Place

Write a number from the box for each clue.

33
48
50
64
76
81

1. I have 4 tens. ________
2. I have 6 ones. ________
3. I have no ones. ________
4. I have 8 tens. ________
5. I have the same number of tens and ones. ________
6. Which number is not used? ________

FAST Math

Add. Circle two sums that are the same.

13	61	39	44	53	27
+ 54	+ 17	+ 50	+ 53	+ 16	+ 42
____	____	____	____	____	____

Think Tank

Jango the goat walks in a line with other goats. There are 12 goats in front of Jango. There are 7 goats behind him. How many goats are in line?

____

Show your work in the tank.

Data Place

The menu shows zoo foods you can buy to feed the animals.

Use the menu to answer the questions.

ZOO FOODS	
Bagels for Bears	40¢
Carrots for Camels	25¢
Lettuce for Llamas	20¢
Leaves for Lambs	15¢
Salmon for Seals	75¢

1. You have 3 quarters. How many carrots can you buy? ______
2. You have 1 dollar. How many llamas can you buy lettuce for? ______

3. You buy salmon for a seal. How much change will you get back from a dollar? ______
4. How much more for salmon than leaves? ______

Puzzler

Long ago, people in Egypt drew pictures to stand for numbers.

1 =	ǀ
10 =	∩
100 =	𓍢

Write the number we use for the value of each picture number. Then write the picture number for our numbers.

 = ______

 = ______

 = ______

14 = ______

40 = ______

200 = ______

JUMPSTART 17

Side A

Name ______________________ Date ______________

Number Place

X the one in each row that does *not* belong.

22	2 tens 2 ones	2 + 2	twenty-two
53	5 tens 3 ones	50 + 3	thirty-five
74	4 tens 7 ones	40 + 7	forty-seven
81	1 ten 8 ones	80 + 1	eighty-one

FAST Math

Regroup 10 ones as 1 ten.

3 tens 12 ones = _4_ tens _2_ ones

4 tens 14 ones = ____ tens ____ ones

5 tens 11 ones = ____ tens ____ ones

6 tens 13 ones = ____ tens ____ ones

2 tens 18 ones = ____ tens ____ ones

7 tens 17 ones = ____ tens ____ ones

Think Tank

Casey is a good baseball player. He threw a baseball 87 feet. Fern's best throw was 15 feet shorter. How far did Fern's best throw go?

_______ feet

Show your work in the tank.

Data Place

Count the tools. Make a bar graph for what you see.

How Many Tools?

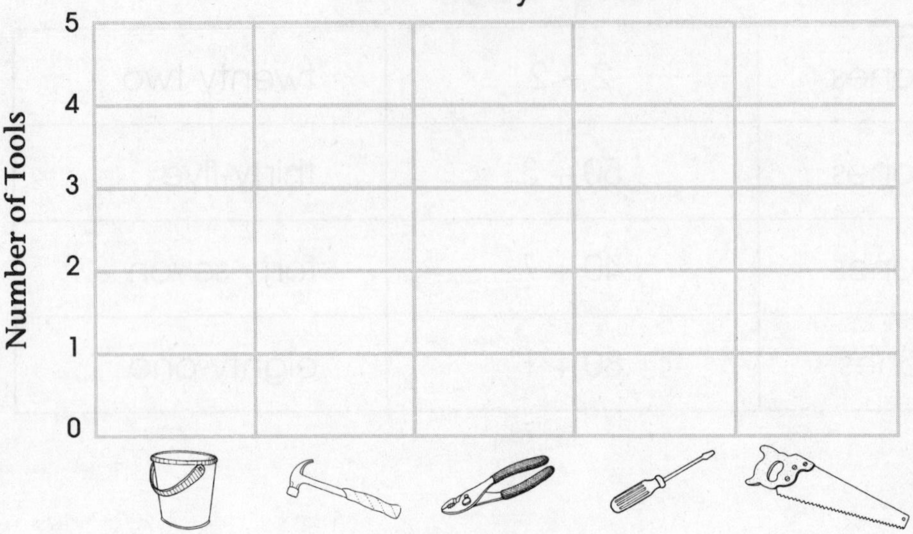

Kind of Tool

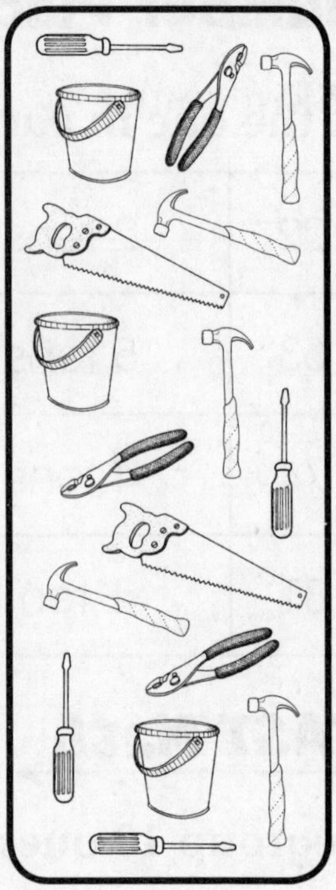

1. How many tools did you count in all? ____________

2. The number of  + the number of 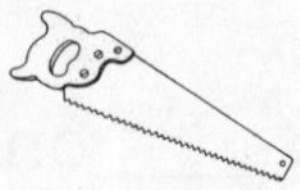 = the number of ________

Puzzler

Each letter on the key pad has a number value.
The name *Jeb* is worth 10. Do you see why?

Find the sum of the letters in:

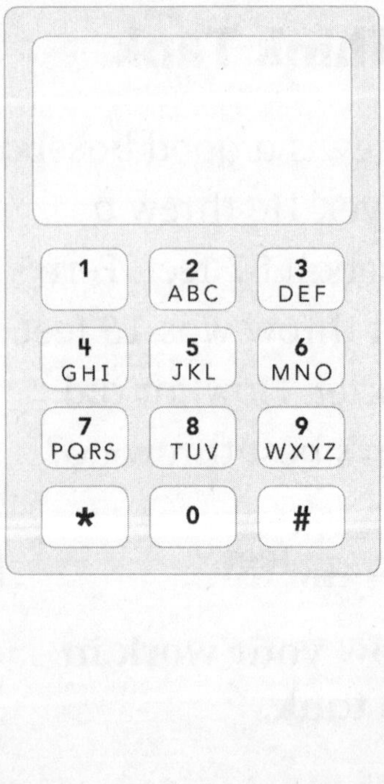

your name. ______________________

a friend's name. ______________________

your school's name. ______________________

the day today. ______________________

your favorite color. ______________________

Name ______________________ Date ______________

Number Place

Skip count by 10s to 100.

10, ____, ____, ____, ____,

____, ____, ____, ____, ____

FAST Math

Add. Regroup as needed. Circle the greatest sum.

48	75	51	36	40	94
+ 36	+ 16	+ 39	+ 49	+ 82	+ 53
____	____	____	____	____	____

Think Tank

Irini has a favorite day of the week. She chose this day because it is the only day that has an *i* in it. What is Irini's favorite day of the week?

____

Show your work in the tank.

Data Place

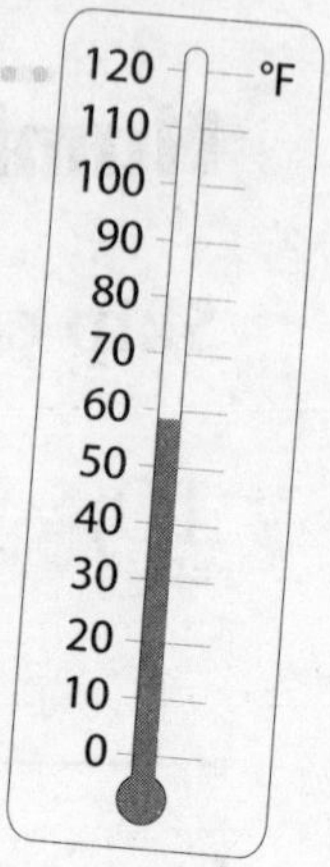

Faye read the temperature outside each day at 1:00 P.M.

Use the calendar to answer the questions.

DAY	Monday	Tuesday	Wednesday	Thursday	Friday
TEMPERATURE	53° F	59° F	62° F	59° F	66° F

1. What was the temperature on Wednesday? ___________
2. Which 2 days had the same temperature? ___________

   ____
3. Which was the warmest day? ___________
4. Which was the coolest day? ___________

Puzzler

Color the picture. Use the key.

Key	
If the number is	**Color the space**
10–19	blue
20–39	red
40–59	yellow
60–79	green
80–99	orange
100 or more	purple

JUMPSTART 19

Side A

Name ______________________ Date ______________

Number Place

Compare. Write < or >.

68 ◯ 86   37 ◯ 29   44 ◯ 40

7 ◯ 81   90 ◯ 85   23 ◯ 32

FAST Math

Round each addend to the nearest 10. Then estimate the sum.

47 → ☐	51 → ☐	72 → ☐
+ 32 → ☐	+ 28 → ☐	+ 19 → ☐
about: ______	about: ______	about: ______

Think Tank

Walid is making a family album. So far, he has 86 photos of his parents. He also has 103 photos of his brothers and sisters. How many photos are in Walid's album?

______ photos

Show your work in the tank.

Data Place

Use the grid to fill in the blanks.

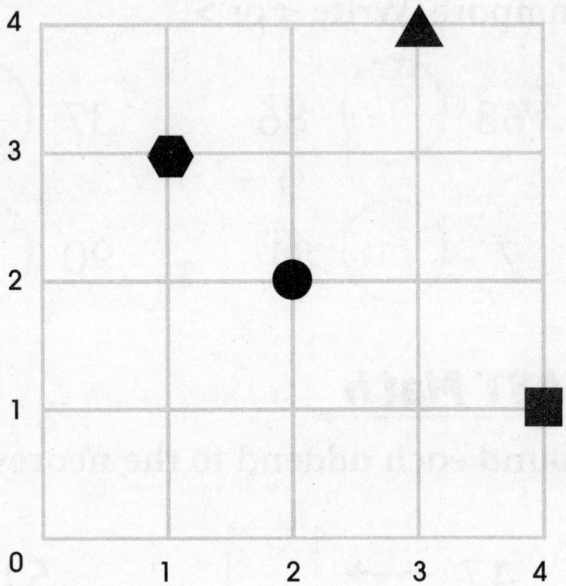

1. To find the ■,

   go *across* _____ and then *up* _____ .

2. To find the ●,

   go *across* _____ and then *up* _____ .

3. To find the ▲,

   go *across* _____ and then *up* _____ .

4. To find the ⬢,

   go *across* _____ and then *up* _____ .

5. Draw a ♥ at (2, 4).

Puzzler

Complete the box maze.

Start at ★.

End at ☾.

Draw a path through each box just *once* without lifting your pencil.

Hint: Try first with a finger.

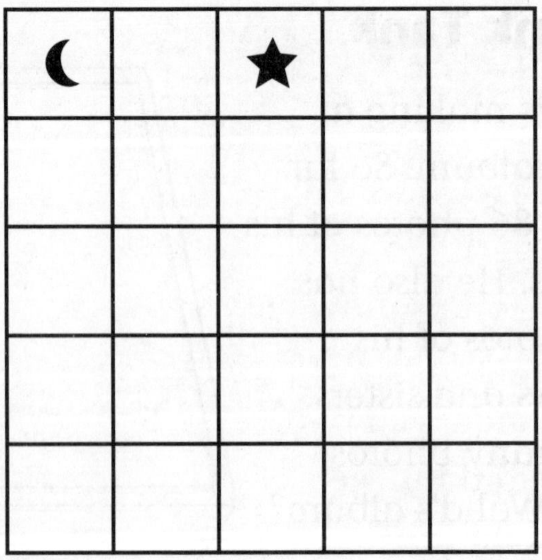

JUMPSTART 20

Side A

Name ______________________ Date ______________

Number Place

Order from *least* to *greatest*.

30, 70, 55, 35 ______________________

62, 67, 60, 70 ______________________

84, 94, 89, 48 ______________________

73, 105, 200, 162 ______________________

FAST Math

Add. Regroup as needed. Circle the greatest sum.

14	25	53	28	53	29
37	52	51	40	18	32
+ 21	+ 16	+ 67	+ 27	+ 25	+ 16
____	____	____	____	____	____

Think Tank

Ruthie went to a diner for lunch. She spent $3.29 for a sandwich and $1.50 for lemonade. How much did Ruthie spend on lunch?

____

Show your work in the tank.

Data Place

Use the graph about favorite ice-cream flavors to answer the questions.

Favorite Ice-Cream Flavors

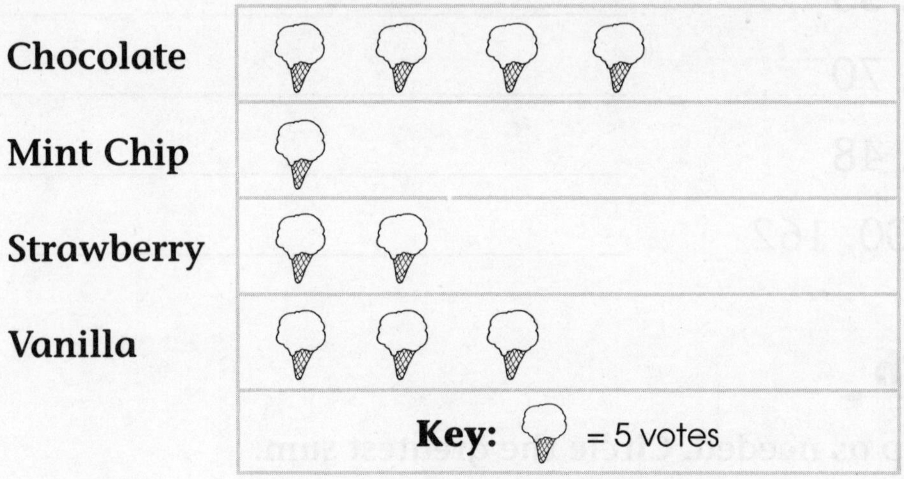

Number of Votes

1. What is the value of one ? ________________
2. How many people like vanilla best? ________________
3. Strawberry? ________________
4. Mint chip? ________________
5. Which was the most popular flavor? ________________
6. How many people picked this flavor? ________________

Puzzler

This magic square uses the digits 1–9 *once* each. The sum of every row ↔, column ↕, and diagonal ↗ or ↘ is 15. Some numbers are in place.

Fill in the rest of the magic square. Start with what you know.

2		
	5	
6		8

JUMPSTART 21

Side A

Name ______________________ Date ______________

Number Place

Order from *greatest* to *least*.

27, 72, 54, 45 ______________________

49, 59, 29, 39 ______________________

83, 38, 33, 88 ______________________

105, 250, 520, 55 ______________________

FAST Math

Subtract. Circle the answer that has 9 ones.

76	68	59	44	83	97
− 54	− 25	− 20	− 13	− 42	− 61
____	____	____	____	____	____

Think Tank

A school chorus has 45 singers. There are 23 boys. How many of the singers are girls?

______ girls

Show your work in the tank.

Data Place

The students at Zoller School took a survey. They were asked what they like to drink when they have a cold. The table shows how kids voted.

Drinks	Votes
Hot Cider	83
Hot Cocoa	149
Chicken Soup	55
Warm Honey Milk	30

Use the results to fill in the blanks.

1. Eighty-three kids voted for ______________________.
2. ______________________ got the most votes.
3. ______________________ got 55 votes.
4. How many more voted for hot cider than warm honey milk? ________

Puzzler

Use each number in the oval. Write it in the box where it belongs. Then make up one more number for each box.

45 12 106 112 129 144
150 99 161 173 188 192 170
203 367 132 7 501

Numbers < 123	Numbers From 124 to 170	Numbers > 170

JUMPSTART 22

Side A

Name ______________________ Date ______________

Number Place

Write the number that is 10 *more*.

6 ______	35 ______	77 ______
208 ______	354 ______	483 ______

Write the number that is 10 *less*.

13 ______	59 ______	86 ______
364 ______	450 ______	712 ______

FAST Math

Regroup 1 ten as 10 ones.

3 tens 2 ones = 2 tens 12 ones	4 tens 4 ones = ____ tens ____ ones
5 tens 6 ones = ____ tens ____ ones	6 tens 3 ones = ____ tens ____ ones
2 tens 7 ones = ____ tens ____ ones	9 tens 1 ones = ____ tens ____ ones

Think Tank

Kiri bought a hamburger for $1.50, salad for $1.20, and iced tea for $1.00. How much did she spend in all?

Kiri spent __________ in all.

Show your work in the tank.

Data Place

Graph the price of each item.

School Supply Prices

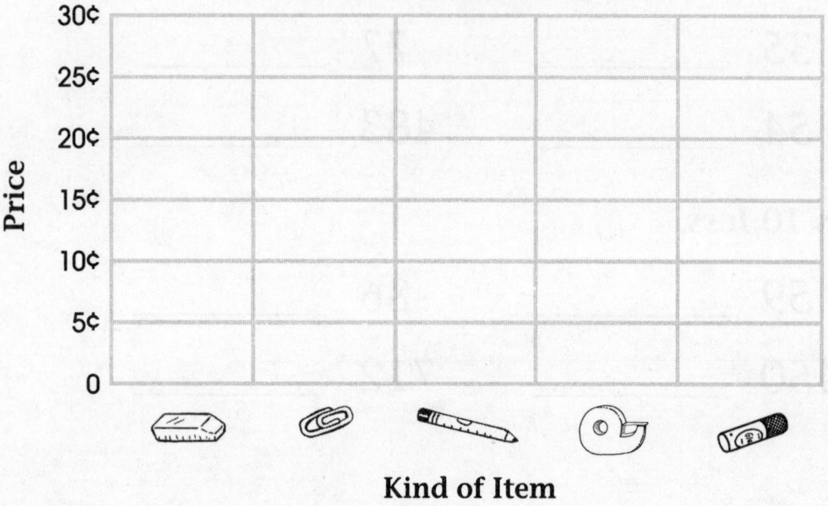

Price List	
Eraser	10¢
Paper Clip	5¢
Pencil	25¢
Tape	20¢
Glue Stick	25¢

1. Which item costs a nickel? ______________________

2. Which item costs a dime? ______________________

3. Which 2 items have the same price? ______________________

____

Puzzler

What do scientists call the part of the world that has the most volcanos?

Use the clues to solve the riddle!

the ___ ___ ___ ___ of ___ ___ ___ ___

The eighth letter is *e*.

The fourth letter is *g*.

The third letter is *n*.

The seventh letter is *r*.

The fifth letter is *f*.

The first letter is *r*.

The sixth letter is *i*.

The second letter is *i*.

JUMPSTART 23

Side A

Name ______________________________ Date ________________

Number Place

Every number in the balloon is *odd* or *even*. Write each number where it belongs.

Odd Numbers	Even Numbers

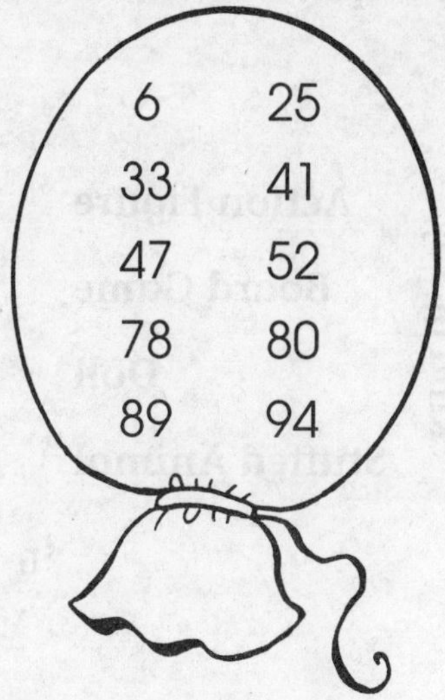

FAST Math

Subtract. Regroup as needed. Circle the difference that is even.

45	63	56	74	81	90
− 28	− 14	− 29	− 37	− 45	− 63
____	____	____	____	____	____

Think Tank

Jake took 5 quarters and 6 dimes to the store. He spent 85¢ on a fruit roll. He spent 50¢ on a banana. How much money does Jake have left?

Jake has __________ left.

Show your work in the tank.

Data Place

Graph the data about favorite toys.

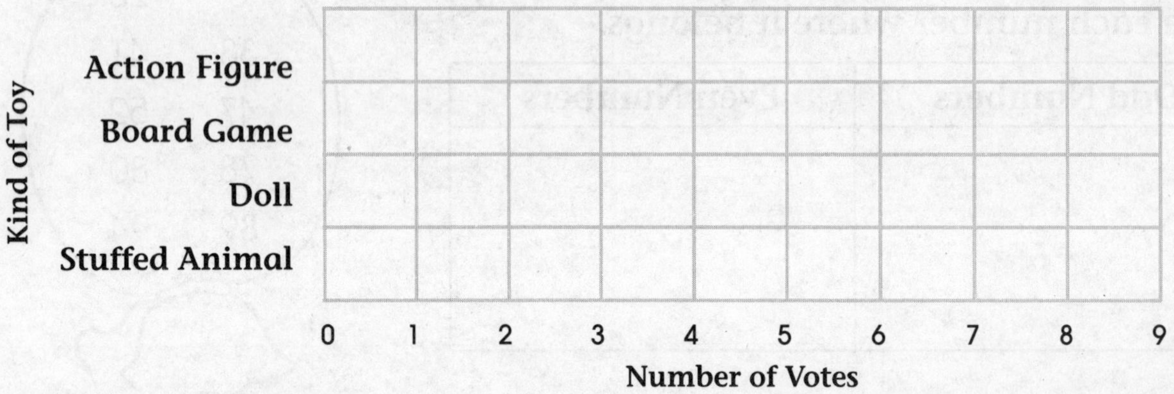

1. Which toy got twice as many votes as a board game? ______________________

2. Which 2 toys got a total of 13 votes?

____

Favorite Toys

Action Figure	卌 II
Doll	卌 I
Stuffed Animal	卌 III
Board Game	IIII

Puzzler

Each number in the tic-tac-toe grid is in a different shape. Do you see why  stands for 7?

Use the code to do the math.

0	1	2
3	4	5
6	7	8

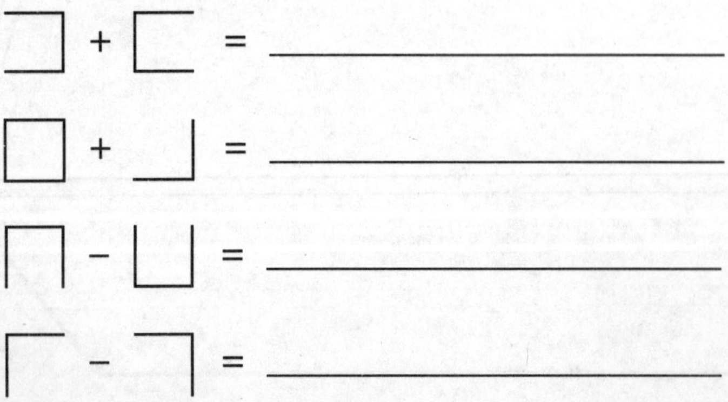

Morning Jumpstarts: Math, Grade 2 © 2013 by Scholastic Teaching Resources

JUMPSTART 24

Side A

Name ____________________ Date ______________

Number Place

Write each money amount with a ¢ sign.

6 pennies =	5 dimes 7 pennies =
1 dime 4 pennies =	8 dimes 9 pennies =
3 dimes 5 pennies =	9 dimes =
4 dimes =	98 pennies =

FAST Math

Round each number to estimate the difference.

78 → ☐	62 → ☐	73 → ☐
− 33 → ☐	− 28 → ☐	− 17 → ☐
about: ______	about: ______	about: ______

Think Tank

Dad is older than 40 and younger than 70. His age is an even number. Its digits add to 9. How old is Dad?

He is ______ years old.

Show your work in the tank.

Data Place

Use the Venn diagram to answer the questions.

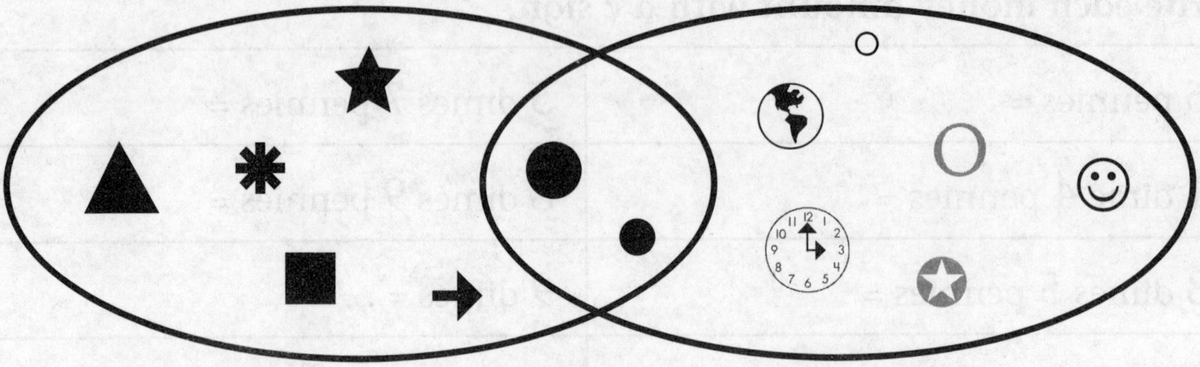

ONLY Black | Black AND Round | ONLY Round

1. How many shapes are ONLY black? ______
2. How many shapes are ONLY round? ______
3. How many shapes are black AND round? ______

Puzzler

Each box has 4 numbers. You can use 3 of them to make an addition or subtraction fact.

X each number that does *not* belong.

120	60	22	300	120	725
70	45	33	500	240	525
50	35	44	600	360	425
40	10	66	800	680	300

JUMPSTART 25

Side A

Name ______________________ Date ______________

Number Place

Round each number to the nearest ten.

24 → ____ 57 → ____ 15 → ____ 81 → ____

72 → ____ 43 → ____ 69 → ____ 96 → ____

FAST Math

Add or subtract. Regroup as needed.
Circle the 3-digit answer.

65	74	94	70	87	19
− 29	+ 18	+ 20	− 36	− 59	+ 66
____	____	____	____	____	____

Think Tank

Lulu has 4 coins. They total 60¢. What coins does Lulu have?

She has ______________

____

____

____

____

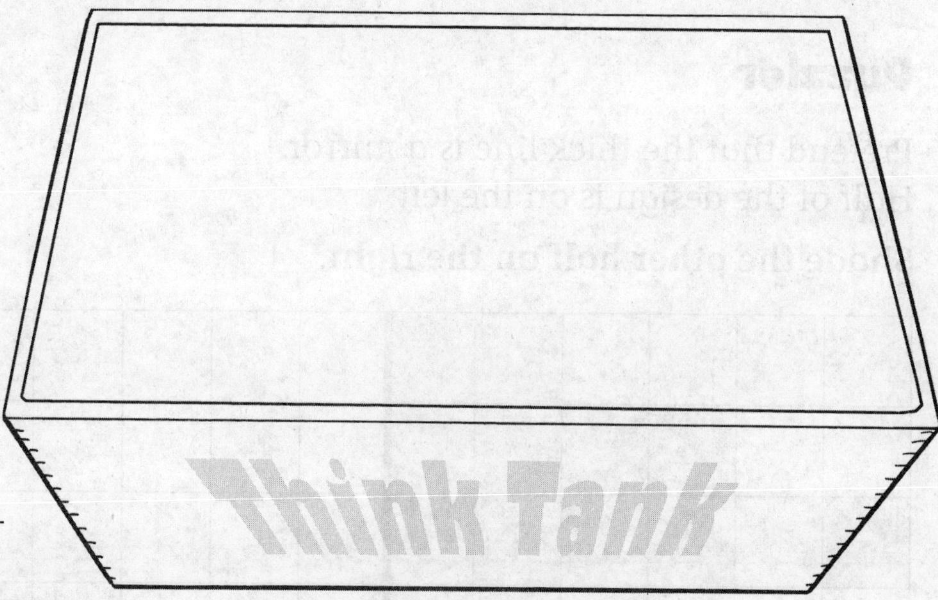

Show your work in the tank.

Data Place

Draw ✔ in the graph for each animal you see.

Animals in the Woods

Butterfly	
Crow	
Rabbit	
Squirrel	
	Key: ✔ = 1 animal

1. How many animals in all? __________

2. How many animals with wings? __________

3. How many more crows than squirrels? __________

Puzzler

Pretend that the thick line is a mirror.
Half of the design is on the left.

Shade the other half on the right.

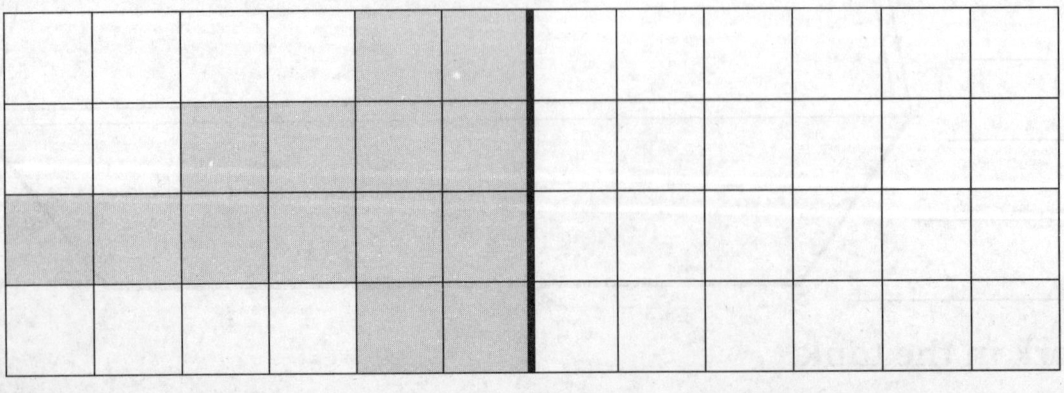

JUMPSTART 26

Side A

Name ______________________ Date ______________

Number Place

Round each money amount to the nearest dime.

27¢ ____	42¢ ____	66¢ ____	88¢ ____
34¢ ____	55¢ ____	71¢ ____	83¢ ____

FAST Math

Count the coins. Write how much.

1.  ______ ¢

2.  ______ ¢

3.  ______ ¢

Think Tank

Daria's book has 96 pages. She read 28 pages on Monday. She read 17 pages on Tuesday. How many more pages are left to read?

________ pages

Show your work in the tank.

Data Place

Al collects old keys. How many of each kind does he have?

Count and tally them in the table.

Al's Old Keys

Key	Tally	Number

1. How many keys in all?

____

2. How many more  than  ?

____

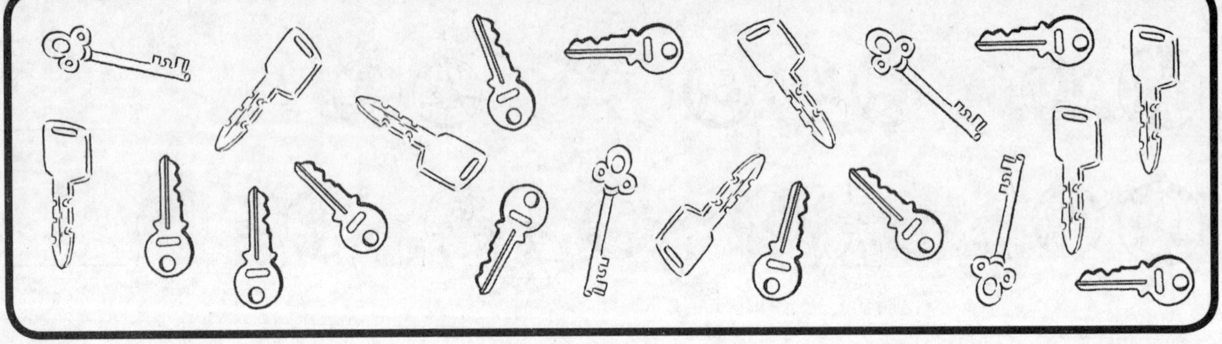

Puzzler

This magic square uses numbers 10 to 18.
The sum in each row ⟷, column ↕, and diagonal ⤢ or ⤡ is 42.

Figure out which numbers are missing. Then write them where they belong.

15	16	11
	14	
17		

JUMPSTART 27 **Side A**

Name ______________________ Date ____________

Number Place

Write the missing numbers.

19, _____ , _____ , _____ , _____ , 24

38, _____ , _____ , _____ , _____ , 43

67, _____ , _____ , _____ , _____ , 72

FAST Math

Round each number to estimate the difference.

66¢ → ☐	72¢ → ☐	93¢ → ☐
– 42¢ → ☐	– 26¢ → ☐	– 48¢ → ☐
about: ______	about: ______	about: ______

Think Tank

There are 50 sticky notes in every pack. Gary gets 4 packs. How many sticky notes does he have? Use mental math to solve. He has

______ sticky notes.

Use the tank if you need to.

Data Place

Use the graph to answer the questions.

Kids' Favorite Rainy Day Activity

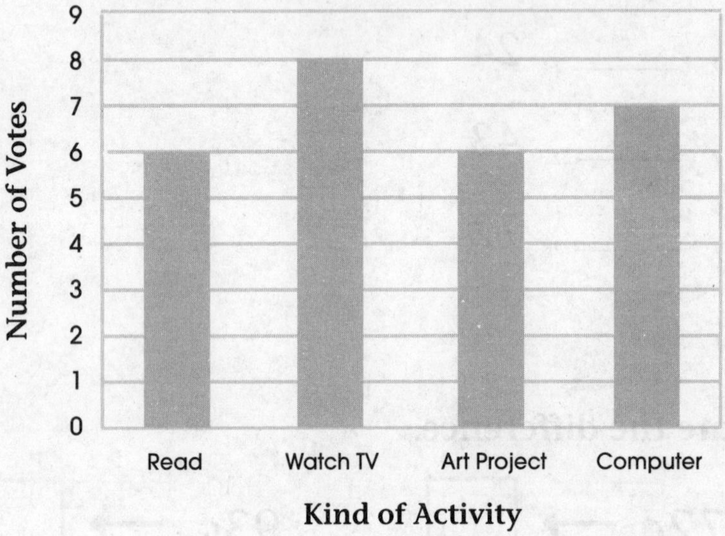

1. Which activities got more than 6 votes? ______________________

____

2. Which 2 activities got the same number of votes? ______________

____

3. How many kids voted in all? ______

Puzzler

Study the pattern in each row. Draw the next shape for each pattern.

JUMPSTART 28

Side A

Name ______________________ Date ______________

Number Place

Count by hundreds.

100, ________, 300, ________, ________,

600, ________, ________, ________, 1,000.

FAST Math

Count the money. Write how much. Use $ and ¢.

1.  ________

2.  ________

3.  ________

Think Tank

A box is 25 inches tall.
You stack up 3 boxes.
How tall is your stack?
The stack is

________ inches tall.

Show your work in the tank.

Data Place

This is how Tim spends Saturday mornings.

What I Do	Start Time
Wake up.	half past seven
Watch cartoons.	quarter to eight
Get dressed.	quarter to ten
Take piano lesson.	quarter after ten
Play with Sparky.	half past eleven

Use the table to write each time in the story.

Tim wakes up at ___7:30___. He watches cartoons starting at __________. He gets dressed at __________. His piano lesson starts at __________. After his lesson, Tim plays with his dog at __________.

Puzzler

Delia stretched 2 rubber bands to make a D on her geoboard.

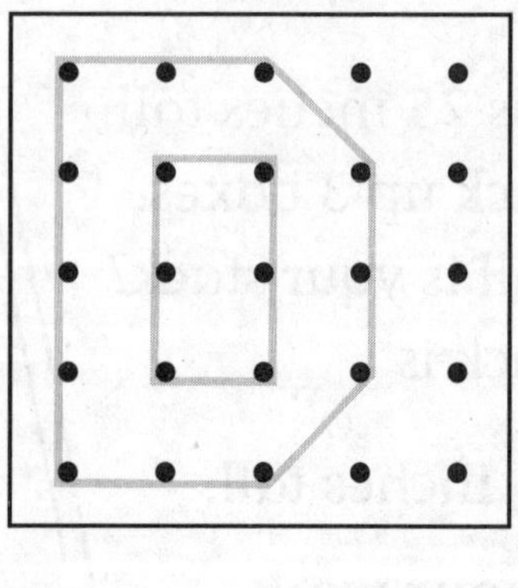

1. How many pins does the outside rubber band touch? __________
2. How many pins does the inside rubber band touch? __________
3. How many pins are *not* used? __________

Name ______________________ Date ______________

Number Place

Write the number to show how many.

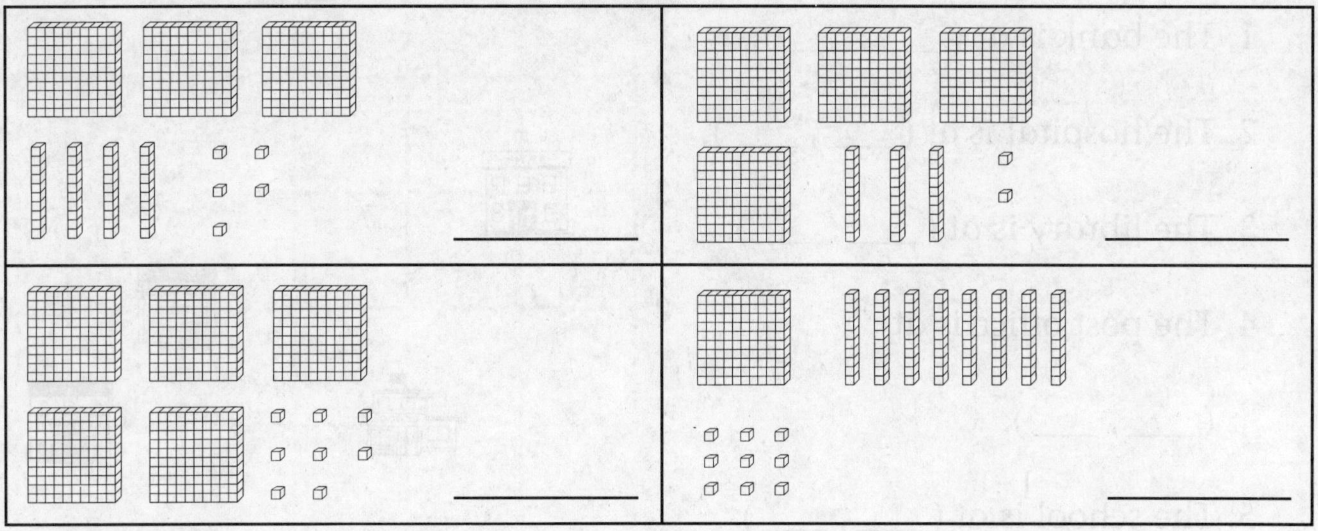

FAST Math

Round to the nearest dollar. Estimate the difference.

\$4.13 → ☐	\$9.28 → ☐	\$7.46 → ☐
– \$1.77 → ☐	– \$5.81 → ☐	– \$3.99 → ☐
about: ______	about: ______	about: ______

Think Tank

I am a solid shape.
I have 6 square faces.
What shape am I?

____

Show your work in the tank.

Data Place

Write the number pair where you find each building.

1. The bank is at (____ , ____).
2. The hospital is at (____ , ____).
3. The library is at (____ , ____).
4. The post office is at
   (____ , ____).
5. The school is at (____ , ____).

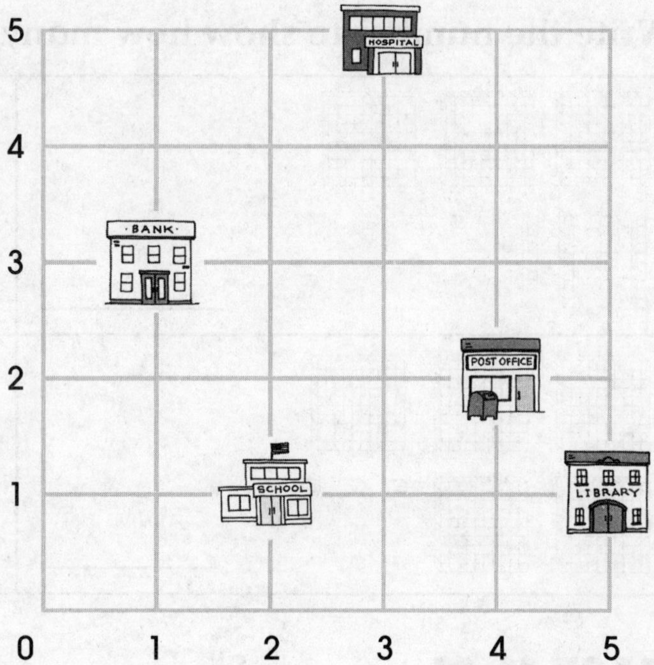

Puzzler

Unscramble the shape words. Use the word bank to check your spelling.

Word Bank		
circle	cone	cube
hexagon	rectangle	sphere
square	triangle	

bceu ______________________ preesh ______________________

enoc ______________________ langerit ______________________

quarsue ______________________ noxhage ______________________

crilec ______________________ grancleet ______________________

Name ______________________ Date ____________

Number Place

Write the number on the line.

Hundreds	Tens	Ones
4	8	7

____

Hundreds	Tens	Ones
9	1	4

____

Hundreds	Tens	Ones
8	9	6

____

Hundreds	Tens	Ones
5	0	2

____

FAST Math

Add or subtract. Use mental math. Circle answers of 700.

400 + 500 = _____ 1,000 – 300 = _____ 300 + 600 = _____

700 – 200 = _____ 800 – 200 = _____ 200 + 500 = _____

Think Tank

A jet has 178 seats. There are 52 seats next to windows. The exit rows have 26 seats. How many other seats does the jet have?

__________ seats

Show your work in the tank.

Data Place

The picture shows parts of a house. Answer the questions about it.

1. Which room is a triangle?

____

2. Which room is above the kitchen?

____

3. Which room is between the kitchen and living room?

____

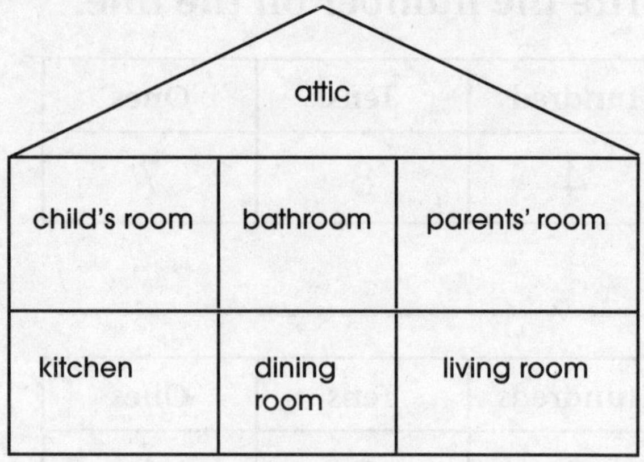

Puzzler

Look at the letters on the grid. Write the word that the number pairs spell.

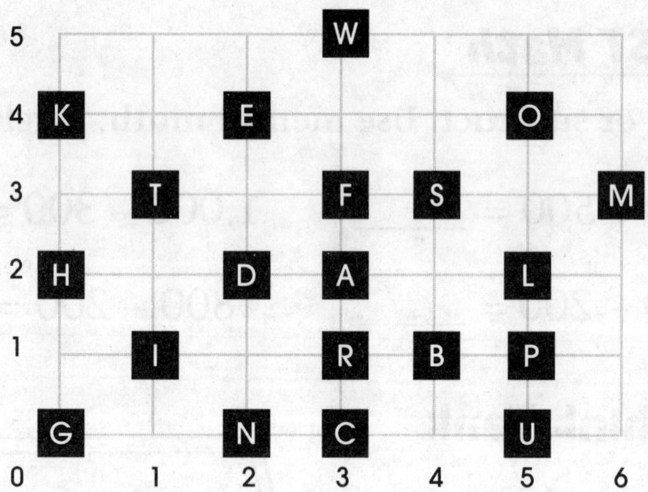

(6, 3) (3, 2) (5, 1) ______________________

(4, 1) (5, 4) (5, 4) (1, 3) ______________________

(2, 2) (5, 0) (3, 0) (0, 4) (4, 3) ______________________

(3, 5) (3, 2) (0, 0) (5, 4) (2, 0) ______________________

(1, 1) (3, 0) (1, 1) (3, 0) (5, 2) (2, 4) ______________________

JUMPSTART 31

Side A

Name ______________________ Date ____________

Number Place

How many hundreds, tens, and ones?

542 = ______ hundreds ______ tens ______ ones

785 = ______ hundreds ______ tens ______ ones

369 = ______ hundreds ______ tens ______ ones

804 = ______ hundreds ______ tens ______ ones

217 = ______ hundreds ______ tens ______ ones

FAST Math

Circle the better length for the real object.

1. 

20 centimeters
OR
20 meters

2. 

3 centimeters
OR
3 meters

3. 

12 centimeters
OR
12 meters

Think Tank

Kit has 87¢. He buys a pen for 45¢. He buys an eraser for 30¢. How much money is left? Kit still has

______________.

Show your work in the tank.

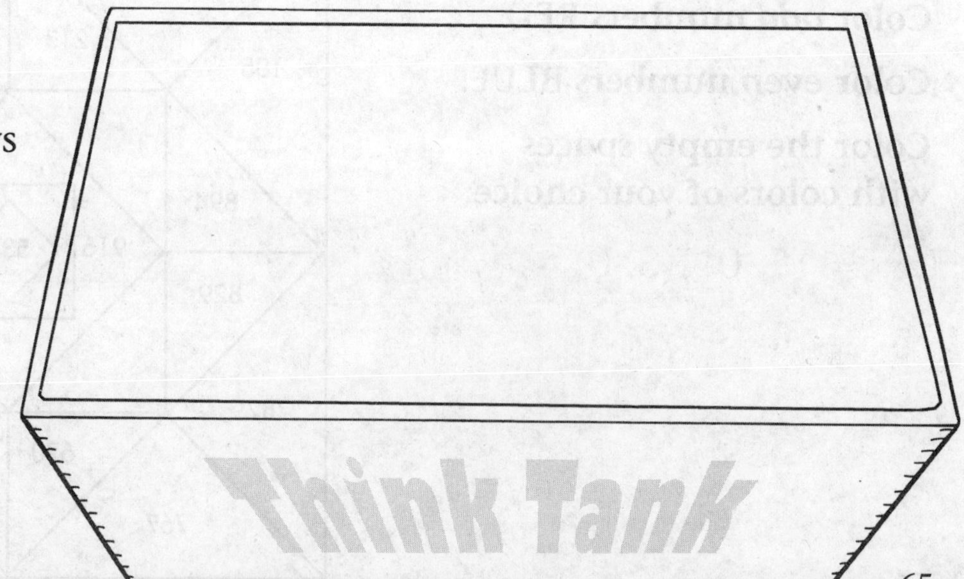

Data Place

Use the calendar to answer the questions.

Weather in March

Sunday	Monday	Tuesday	Wednesday	Thursday	Friday	Saturday
	1	2	3	4	5	6
7	8	9	10	11	12	13

1. How many days had snow? _______
2. How many days were sunny? _______
3. How many more cloudy days than rainy days? _______
4. What was the weather on March 6? ____________________
5. Which school day had snow? ____________________
6. Why is the top left box blank? ____________________

Puzzler

Color *odd* numbers RED.

Color *even* numbers BLUE.

Color the empty spaces with colors of your choice.

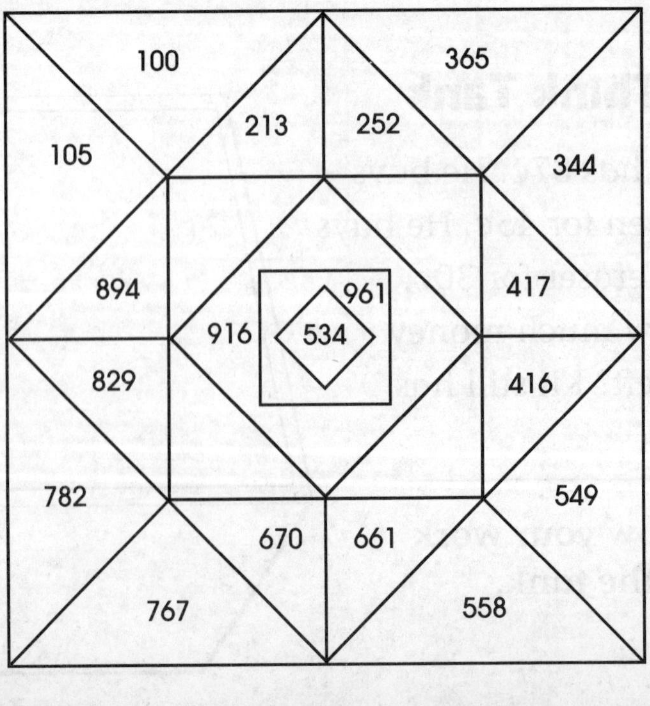

JUMPSTART 32

Side A

Name ______________________________ Date ______________

Number Place

Write in standard form.

6 hundreds 3 tens 5 ones = __________

8 hundreds 1 ten 4 ones = __________

5 hundreds 7 tens 2 ones = __________

3 hundreds 9 tens 0 ones = __________

FAST Math

Add. Circle the sum that has digits in counting order.

341	632	396	444	827	234
+ 517	+ 145	+ 502	+ 253	+ 162	+ 555
____	____	____	____	____	____

Think Tank

Draw a big square in the tank. Draw a circle *inside* the square. Draw a triangle *inside* the circle. How many straight lines did you draw?

____

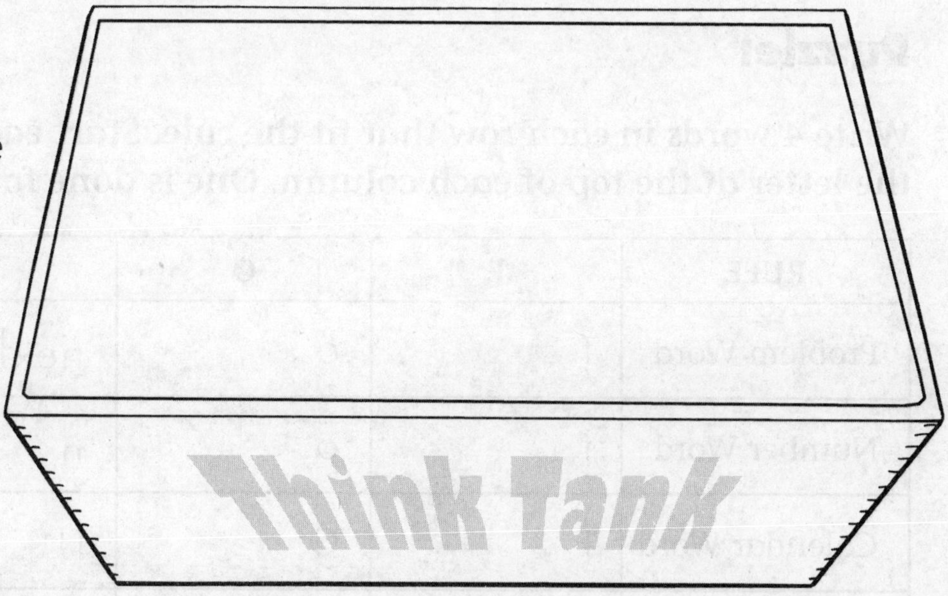

Data Place

Use the table about prices at Costume Closet to answer the questions.

Sale at Costume Closet

Item	Price
Clown Wig	$7
Fake Teeth	$3
Long Cape	$14
Magic Wand	$2
Witch Hat	$5

1. Which item costs the most? ____________________
2. Kisha buys a clown wig and fake teeth.
   How much does she spend? ____________
3. Tomás spends $14 on 3 different items.
   What does he get? ____________________

Puzzler

Write 4 words in each row that fit the rule. Start each word with the letter at the top of each column. One is done for you.

RULE	F	O	N	T
Problem Word	f	o	next	t
Number Word	f	o	n	t
Calendar Word	F	O	N	T
Math Word	f	o	n	t

JUMPSTART 33

Side A

Name ____________________ Date ____________

Number Place

Write each number in expanded form.

734 = ______________________

291 = ______________________

568 = ______________________

439 = ______________________

FAST Math

Regroup 10 tens as 1 hundred.

4 hundreds 16 tens = ______ hundreds ______ tens

7 hundreds 17 tens = ______ hundreds ______ tens

3 hundreds 15 tens = ______ hundreds ______ tens

6 hundreds 14 tens = ______ hundreds ______ tens

Think Tank

Avery buys a sweater for $14. He pays with a $20 bill. How much change does he get?

He gets ________.

Show your work in the tank.

Think Tank

JUMPSTART 33

Side B

Data Place

Three friends sort and count their marble collections.

	Solid	Swirly	Clear
Diego	37	35	16
Layla	18	52	24
Mason	25	31	23

Use the data in the table to answer the questions.

1. How many kinds of marbles do the friends have? ____________
2. Who has the most marbles? ____________
3. Who has more solid marbles than swirly ones? ____________
4. Who has about 30 swirly marbles? ____________

Puzzler

Start at the left. Do what the arrow says to find the next number. (Use the key.) Write the number in the box. Keep going to the end of the row.

Key

- (white arrow) add 20
- (gray arrow) subtract 10
- (black arrow) subtract 100

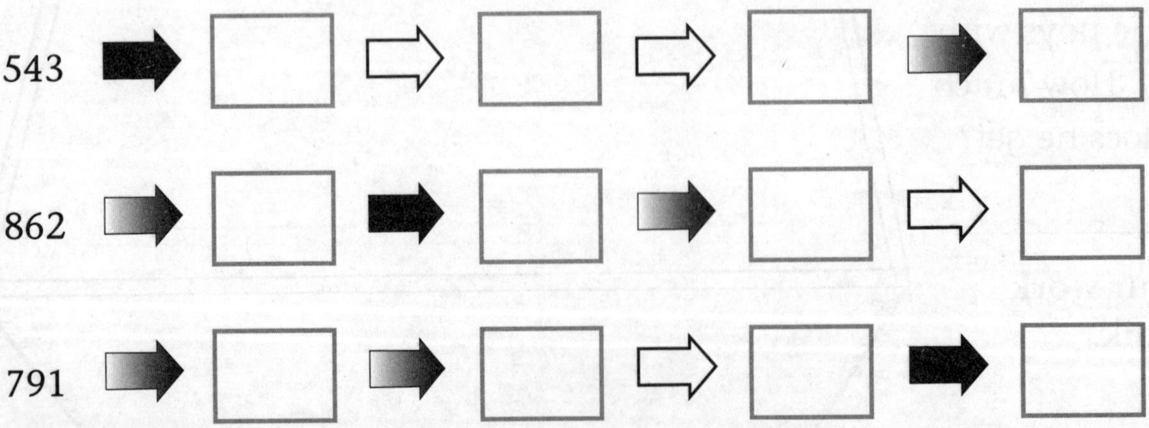

JUMPSTART 34

Side A

Name ____________________ Date ____________

Number Place

Write the value of the underlined digit.

6$\underline{2}$8 ____________ $\underline{6}$04 ____________

$\underline{7}$50 ____________ 14$\underline{9}$ ____________

89$\underline{3}$ ____________ 3$\underline{8}$5 ____________

FAST Math

Add. Regroup 10 ones as 1 ten. Circle the *even* answers.

$$\begin{array}{r} 428 \\ +\ 359 \\ \hline \end{array} \quad \begin{array}{r} 523 \\ +\ 268 \\ \hline \end{array} \quad \begin{array}{r} 627 \\ +\ 254 \\ \hline \end{array} \quad \begin{array}{r} 308 \\ +\ 456 \\ \hline \end{array} \quad \begin{array}{r} 545 \\ +\ 128 \\ \hline \end{array} \quad \begin{array}{r} 369 \\ +\ 315 \\ \hline \end{array}$$

Think Tank

Amos has 26 cards. Zadie has 18 cards. After Amos gives Zadie some cards, they both have the same number of cards. How many cards did Amos give Sadie?

____

Show your work in the tank.

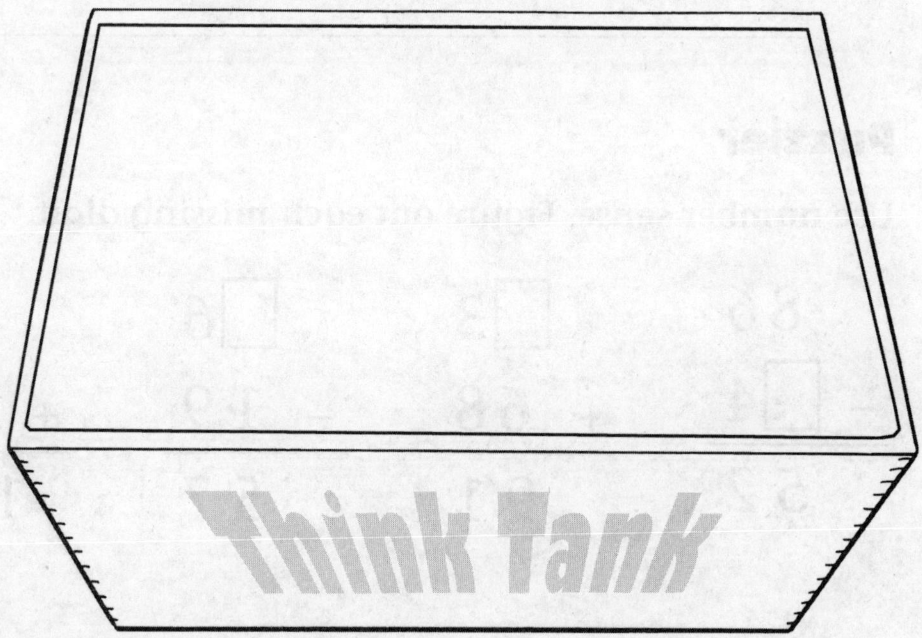

Data Place

Use the table to answer the questions about the weights of 4 sheep at the state fair.

Sheep	Weight in Pounds
Bleep	182
Curly	194
Fluff	177
Snowball	173

1. Write the names of the sheep in order from heaviest to lightest.

   ____

   ____

   ____

2. How much more does the heaviest sheep weigh than the lightest sheep? ______________

3. Which 2 sheep are closest in weight?

   ____

4. Curly got first prize. Why do you think Curly won?

   ____

Puzzler

Use number sense. Figure out each missing digit.

86	□3	□6	3□	90
− □4	+ 68	− 19	+ 81	− 7□
52	91	57	120	14

JUMPSTART 35

Side A

Name ______________________ Date ______________

Number Place

Write a number from the balloon for each clue.

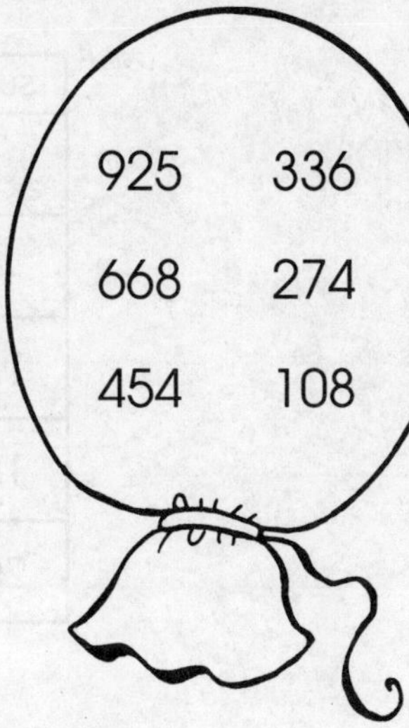

I have 3 hundreds. ________

I have 7 tens. ________

I have no tens. ________

I have 5 ones. ________

I have as many ones as hundreds. ________

Which number is not used? ________

FAST Math

Add. Regroup 10 tens as 1 hundred. Circle the *odd* answers.

240	363	495	563	645	382
+ 388	+ 263	+ 354	+ 176	+ 271	+ 454
____	____	____	____	____	____

Think Tank

Hiram runs a hot dog stand. At 1:30, he left a sign. It said, "I'll be back in 20 minutes." What time will Hiram get back?

____

Show your work in the tank.

Data Place

Use the calendar to answer the questions.

NOVEMBER

SUN	MON	TUE	WED	THU	FRI	SAT
				1	2	3
4	5	6	7	8	9	10
11	12	13	14	15	16	17
18	19	20	21	22	23	24
25	26	27	28	29	30	

1. What day of the week is November 1? ____________________
2. How many days does November have in all? ____________________
3. Election Day is on the first Tuesday of November. What date is Election Day? ____________________
4. Grandpa is coming to visit on December 2. What day of the week will that be? ____________________

Puzzler

Otis raises cows and chickens. Cows have 4 legs. Chickens have 2 legs. One day, Otis counts 26 legs in the yard. He sees 1 more chicken than he sees cows. How many of each animal does Otis see?

Hints:
- Guess and check.
- Make a list.
- Draw a picture.

________ chickens and ________ cows

JUMPSTART 36

Side A

Name ______________________ Date ______________

Number Place

Write in number form.

three hundred seventy-eight ________ five hundred sixty-one ________

four hundred thirty-nine ________ six hundred eleven ________

nine hundred ninety ________ one hundred five ________

FAST Math

Round each addend to the nearest 100. Estimate the sum.

471 → ☐	284 → ☐	528 → ☐
– 316 → ☐	– 509 → ☐	– 382 → ☐
about: ______	about: ______	about: ______

Think Tank

Jonas got a kitten last spring. He named her for the month when he got her. It is the month with the shortest name. What did Jonas name his kitten?

____

Show your work in the tank.

Data Place

Use the table to answer the questions about the seasons in which children have their birthdays.

	Winter	Spring	Summer	Fall
1st Graders	12	17	23	10
2nd Graders	16	18	21	14
3rd Graders	9	19	24	13

1. How many children were born in winter? ______________

2. The season with the most birthdays is ______________.

3. The fewest 3rd graders were born in ______________.

4. The fewest 1st graders were born in ______________.

Puzzler

Each letter has a number value. Use the code to find the value of each word. Add the numbers to get the sums.

A = 1	B = 2	C = 3	D = 4	E = 5	F = 6	G = 7
H = 8	I = 9	J = 10	K = 11	L = 12	M = 13	N = 14
O = 15	P = 16	Q = 17	R = 18	S = 19	T = 20	U = 21
V = 22	W = 23	X = 24	Y = 25	Z = 26		

1. CODE ______________

2. your first name ______________

3. Write your own word. ______________

Solve it. ______________

Name ____________________ Date ____________

Number Place

Write all the missing numbers.

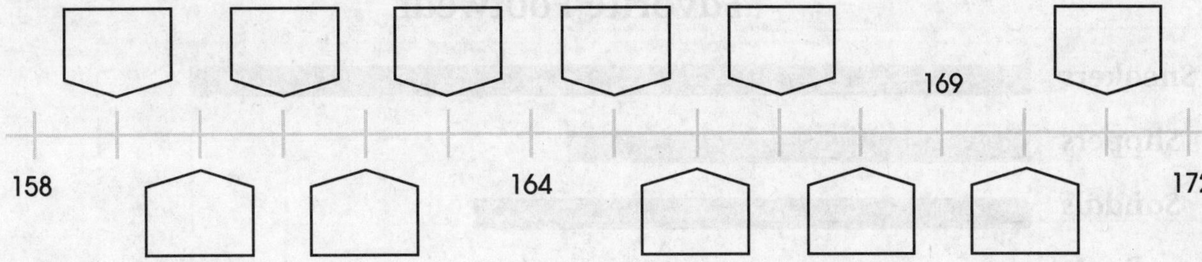

FAST Math

Add. Regroup as needed. Circle the greatest sum.

415	285	203	316	253	514
239	312	181	481	193	368
+ 141	+ 160	+ 545	+ 52	+ 212	+ 107
____	____	____	____	____	____

Think Tank

Today is September 6. Laura will go to Mexico in 2 weeks and 2 days. On what date will Laura begin her trip?

____

____

SEPTEMBER

SUN	MON	TUE	WED	THU	FRI	SAT
				1	2	3
4	5	6	7	8	9	10
11	12	13	14	15	16	17
18	19	20	21	22	23	24
25	26	27	28	29	30	

Data Place

Use the graph about people's favorite footwear to answer the questions.

Favorite Footwear

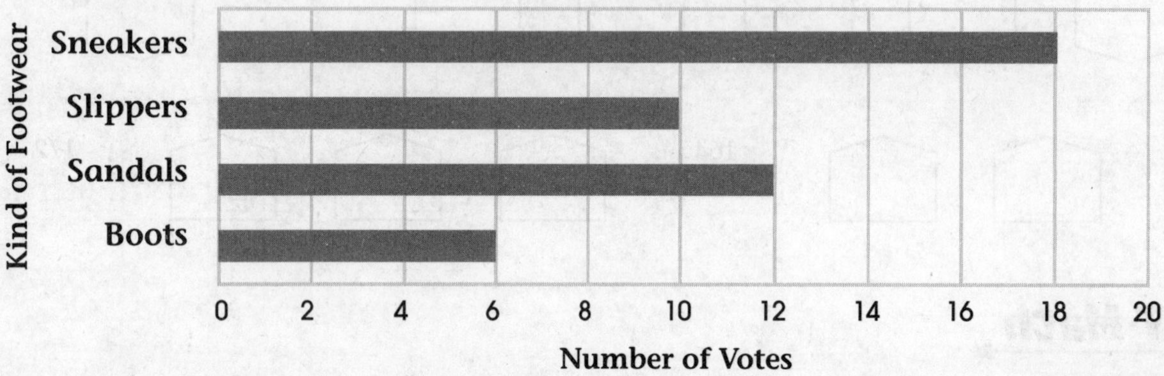

1. How many people like boots best? ___________
2. How many people like sandals best? ___________
3. How many more like sandals than slippers? ___________
4. Which 2 kinds of footwear got as many votes as sneakers?

_______________ and _______________

Puzzler

Use these 4 number cards. List *every* 3-digit number you can make that is less than 583. Write the numbers in the box.

8	3	0	5

Circle the *greatest* number. Underline the *least* number.

JUMPSTART 38

Side A

Name ______________________ Date ____________

Number Place

Write all the missing numbers.

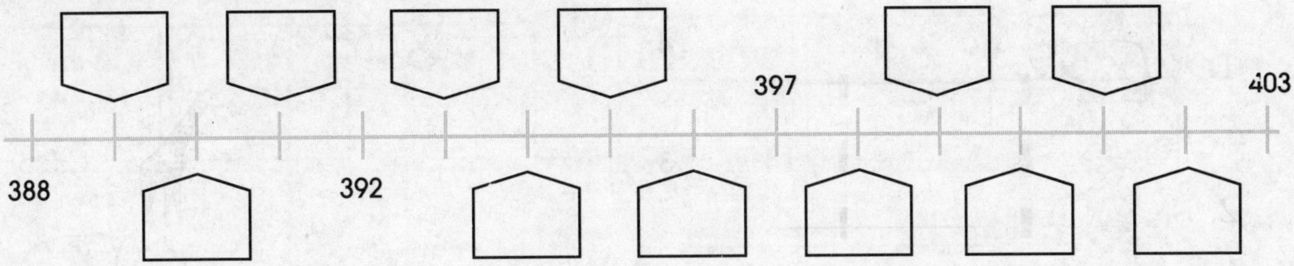

FAST Math

Subtract. Circle the answer that has all digits the same.

948	674	832	765	579	826
− 517	− 201	− 512	− 543	− 146	− 116
____	____	____	____	____	____

Think Tank

Look at the 3 solid shapes in the tank. Which one does *not* belong with the others? Explain why on the lines in the tank.

Data Place

Write the number pair where you find each animal.

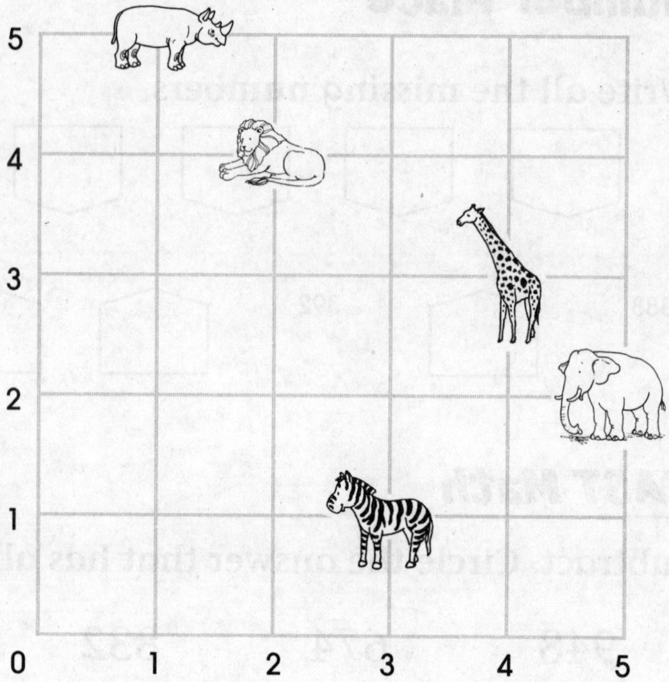

1.  ____________

2.  ____________

3.  ____________

4.  ____________

5. What do you see at (3, 1)? ______________________

Puzzler

Which is the greater sum?

all of the numbers *outside* the circle or all of the numbers *outside* the triangle?

The numbers outside the

____

have the greater sum.

How much greater? ________

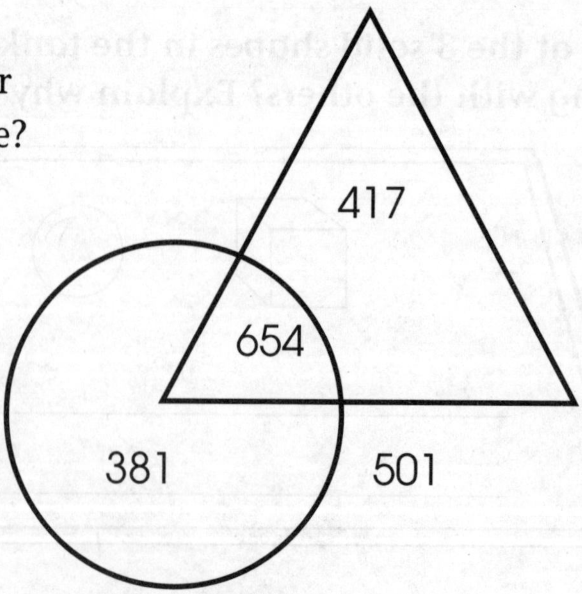

JUMPSTART 39

Side A

Name ______________________ Date ______________

Number Place

Count back by 100.

943, ______, ______, ______, ______,

______, ______, ______, ______, 43

FAST Math

Regroup 1 hundred as 10 tens.

5 hundreds 7 tens = ______ hundreds ______ tens

8 hundreds 6 tens = ______ hundreds ______ tens

2 hundreds 5 tens = ______ hundreds ______ tens

4 hundreds 3 tens = ______ hundreds ______ tens

9 hundreds 0 tens = ______ hundreds ______ tens

Think Tank

A band gave 3 shows. Friday's show had 135 fans. Saturday's show had 241 fans. Sunday's show had 223 fans. How many fans in all heard the band?

____

Show your work in the tank.

Data Place

Draw tallies or write numbers to finish the table about books.

How Many Books Were Read Last Year?

Books	Tally	Number
None	II	
1 to 5		6
6-10	𝍸 𝍸 II	
11-15		15
16 or more		8

1. Last year, how many people read no books? ___________
2. How many read 6 to 10 books? ___________
3. How many read 16 or more books? ___________

Puzzler

Each ◆ = 1 dart. Write the score each dartboard shows.

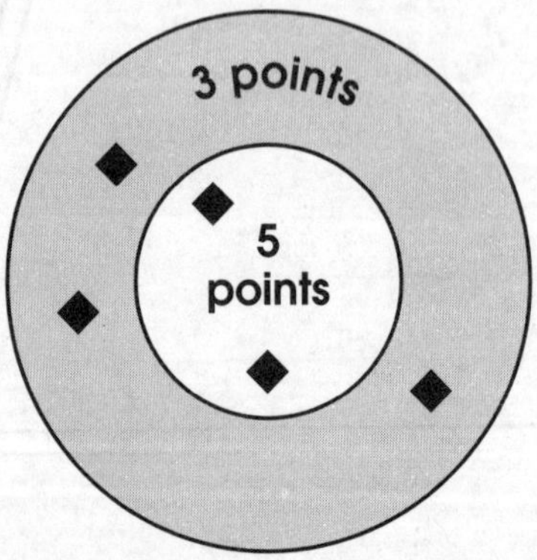

Score: _________

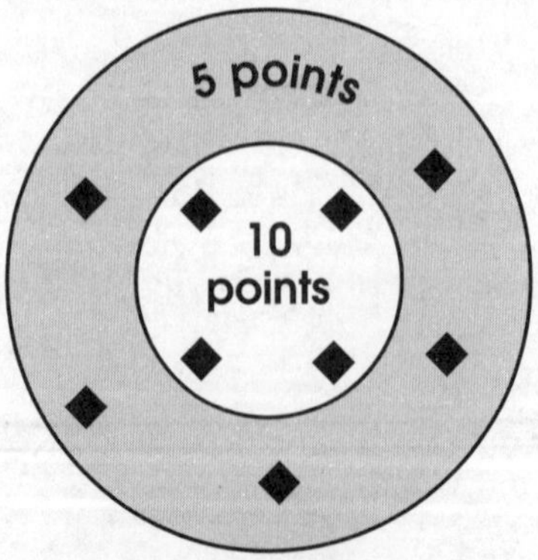

Score: _________

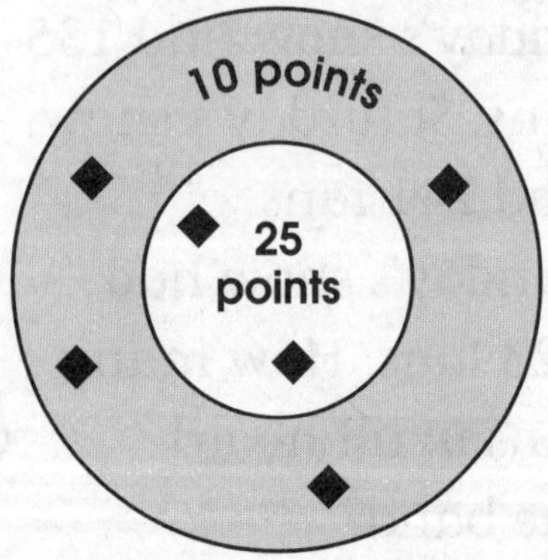

Score: _________

Name ______________________ Date ______________

Number Place

Write the number that comes just *after*.

346, ______	480, ______	797, ______
808, ______	531, ______	959, ______

FAST Math

Subtract. Regroup as needed. Circle the *even* answers.

864	672	836	761	575	823
− 317	− 445	− 408	− 528	− 239	− 716
______	______	______	______	______	______

Think Tank

Jay is 20 years old. Vera is half Jay's age. How old is Vera?

____

Richie is half Vera's age. How old is Richie?

____

Show your work in the tank.

JUMPSTART 40

Side B

Data Place

Paulo jumps on his trampoline every day. He counts his jumps.

Make a bar graph to show Paulo's jumps each day.

Paulo's Jumps	
Monday	25
Tuesday	40
Wednesday	50
Thursday	45
Friday	35

Paulo's Jumps

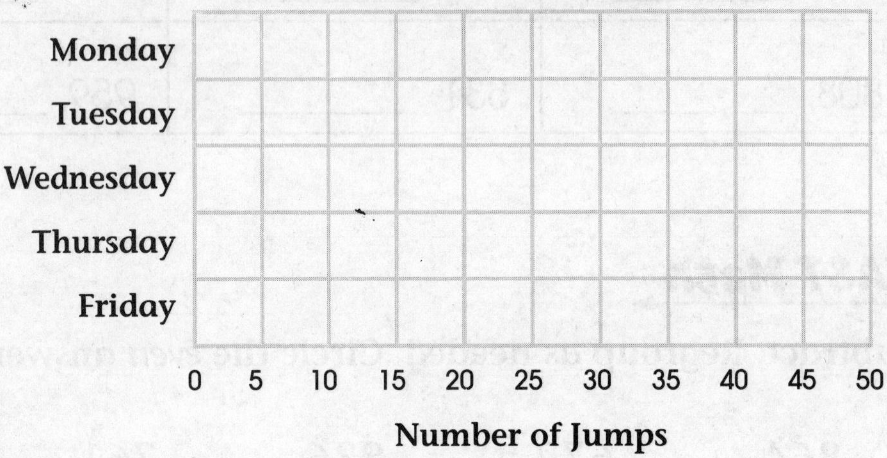

Find the difference between *most* and *least* jumps. ________

Puzzler

For each circle, color *halves* red. Color *thirds* yellow. Color *fourths* blue.

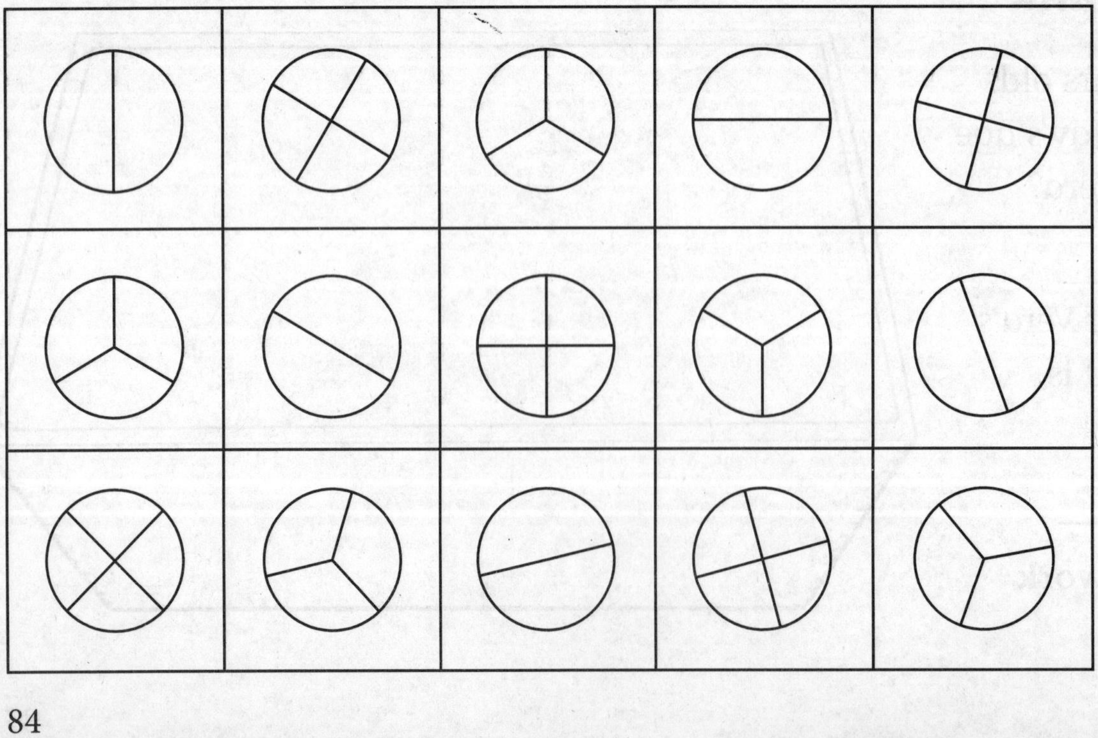

Name ______________________ Date ______________

Number Place

Write the number that comes just *before*.

________ , 734	________ , 139	________ , 909
________ , 528	________ , 647	________ , 460

FAST Math

Subtract. Regroup as needed. Circle the *odd* answers.

867	648	719	936	585	404
– 597	– 175	– 365	– 486	– 294	– 122
____	____	____	____	____	____

Think Tank

A ferry boat can safely carry 85 cars. It can also carry 298 people. How many more people than cars can ride on the ferry?

____

Show your work in the tank.

JUMPSTART 41

Side B

Data Place

The table shows how many people rented skates at the ice rink.

Use the data to answer the questions.

Day	Skates Rented
Thursday	187
Friday	246
Saturday	351
Sunday	321

1. How many people rented skates on Thursday? ___________

2. How many people rented skates on the busiest day? ___________

3. On what day did *about* 250 people rent skates? ___________

4. How many fewer people rented skates on Sunday than on Saturday? Use mental math to find out. ___________

Puzzler

You have 1 of each coin. How many different amounts can you make using just 2 coins? Using just 3 coins?

List all of the amounts below. Draw pictures or use play coins to help you.

Money Amounts With 2 Coins	Money Amounts With 3 Coins

JUMPSTART 42

Side A

Name ______________________ Date ______________

Number Place

Write the number that comes *between*.

245, ______ , 247	272, ______ , 274	147, ______ , 149
623, ______ , 625	564, ______ , 566	808, ______ , 810
479, ______ , 481	799, ______ , 801	966, ______ , 968

FAST Math

Add or subtract. Regroup as needed. Circle the least answer.

86	65	279	345	462	501
− 49	+ 73	− 196	+ 638	− 207	+ 289
______	______	______	______	______	______

Think Tank

Terry has 7 coins. He has no quarters or pennies. He has 1 more of one kind of coin than of the other kind. How much money could Terry have? Find 2 different answers.

1. ________ 2. ________

Show your work in the tank.

Data Place

1. Count by 5s to 30. Write the numbers you say.

____

2. Count by 2s to 30. Write the numbers you say.

____

3. Write all the numbers where they go in the Venn diagram.

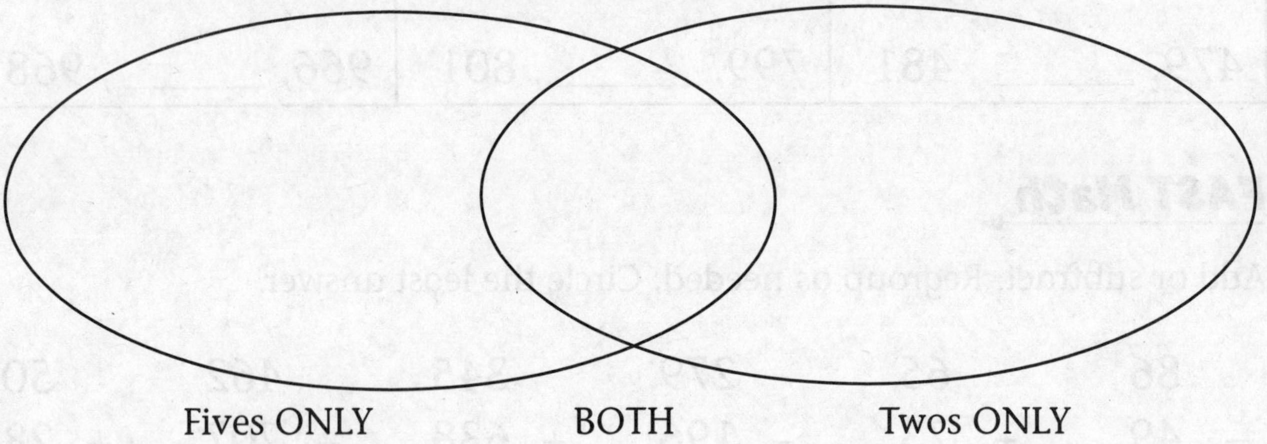

Puzzler

A big window has 25 panes (boxes). Parts of the window are shown below. →

Write in the missing numbers.

1	2	3	4	5
6	7	8	9	10
11	12	13	14	15
16	17	18	19	20
21	22	23	24	25

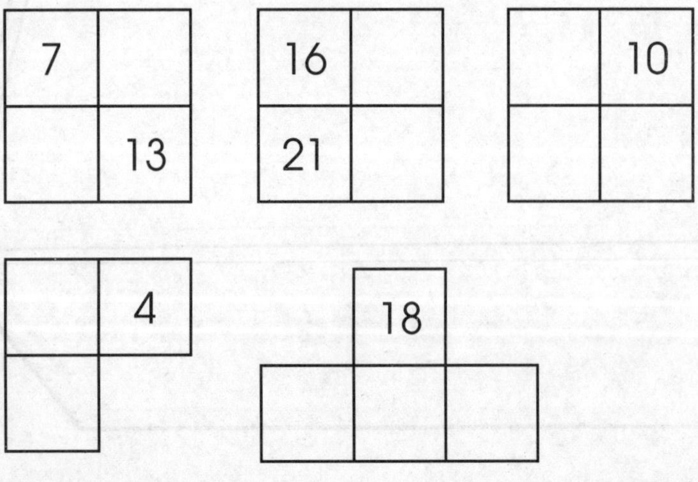

Name ____________________________ Date ________________

Number Place

Compare. Write **<** or **>** .

681	◯	816	371	◯	317	402	◯	420
705	◯	689	908	◯	899	882	◯	891

FAST Math

Add or subtract money. Circle the answer that rounds to $4.

\$5.52	\$3.78	\$8.14	\$6.95	\$7.40
− \$2.08	+ \$1.81	− \$5.60	+ \$2.43	− \$3.90
______	______	______	______	______

Think Tank

A train has 50 seats in each car. The engine pulls 8 cars. How many people in all can ride this train?

____

Use mental math to solve.

Use the tank if you need to.

JUMPSTART 43

Side B

Data Place

Use the table about animal teeth to answer the questions.

1. How many teeth does a lion have? ______

2. Which animal has 5 more teeth than a lion has?

______

3. Which 2 animals have the same number of teeth?

______

How Many Teeth?

Animal	Teeth
Bear 	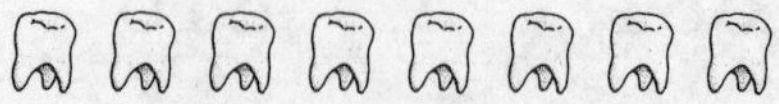
Camel 	
Horse 	
Lion 	
	Key: 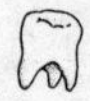 = 5 teeth

4. How many teeth does each of the 2 animals in #3 have? ______

Puzzler

Write a letter from the code to make each number sentence true.

A = 30	E = 10	I = 20	O = 40	U = 50	Y = 60

1. 74 + ______ = 94

2. ______ – 25 = 25

3. ______ + 38 = 68

4. 130 – ______ = 120

5. 7 + ______ = 47

6. 100 – 40 = ______

JUMPSTART 44

Side A

Name ______________________________ Date ________________

Number Place

Order from *least* to *greatest*.

530, 405, 545, 354 ______________________________

819, 914, 814, 948 ______________________________

783, 875, 728, 857 ______________________________

462, 467, 470, 460 ______________________________

FAST Math

Color each fraction.

one third

one half

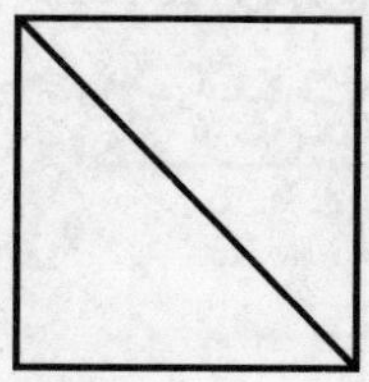

one fourth

the whole

Think Tank

Write the next 2 numbers in each number pattern. Use the tank to figure out the rules.

2, 8, 14, 20,

______ , ______

21, 32, 43, 54,

______ , ______

JUMPSTART 44 **Side B**

Data Place

Count and tally every vowel in the tongue twister.

Pippa pastes pictures of playful purple people.

Vowel	Tally	Number
a		
e		
i		
o		
u		

How many vowels in all are in the tongue twister? ______

Puzzler

Each number is inside a different angle in the **X** code. Can you see why ∧ means 8?
Use the code to figure out each year.

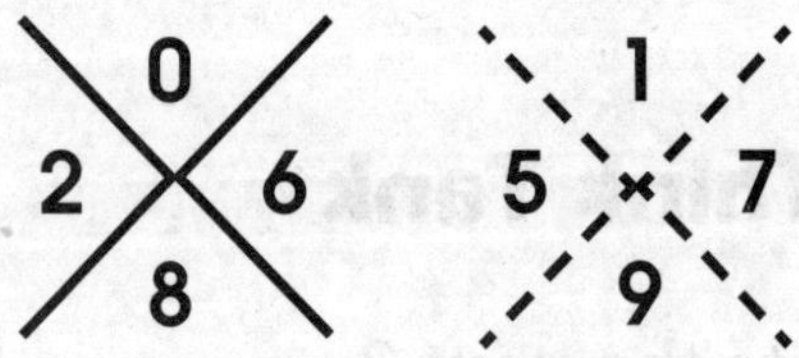

First Thanksgiving  ______

Walt Disney born  ______

First sunglasses sold 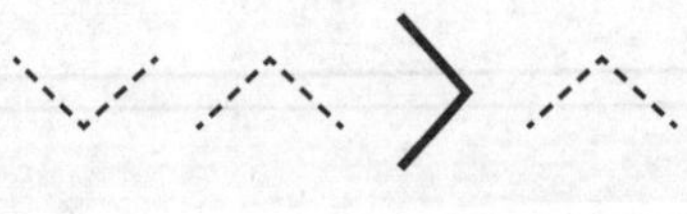 ______

First plastic sandwich bag 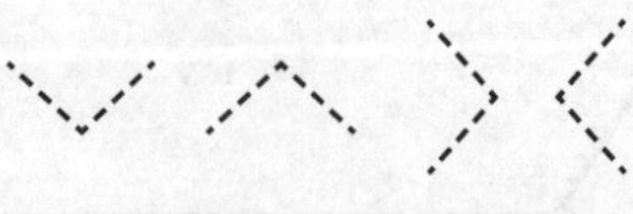 ______

JUMPSTART 45

Side A

Name ______________________ Date ______________

Number Place

Use the number cards.
Write the *greatest* number in the chart.
Write the *least* number in the chart.

4	1	7

	Hundreds	Tens	Ones
Greatest			
Least			

FAST Math

Write the fraction for each shaded part.

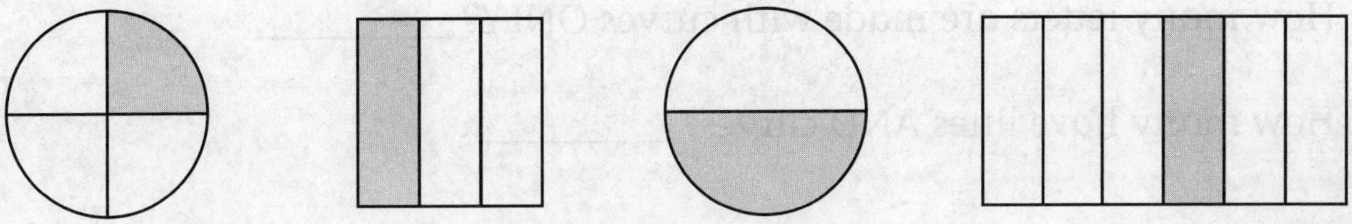

______ ______ ______ ______

Think Tank

Eva buys a turkey wrap for $3.75. She also gets cole slaw for $1.50. She drinks water, which is free. How much does Eva spend in all?

______

Show your work in the tank.

Data Place

Finish the Venn diagram. Write capital letters O to Z where they belong.

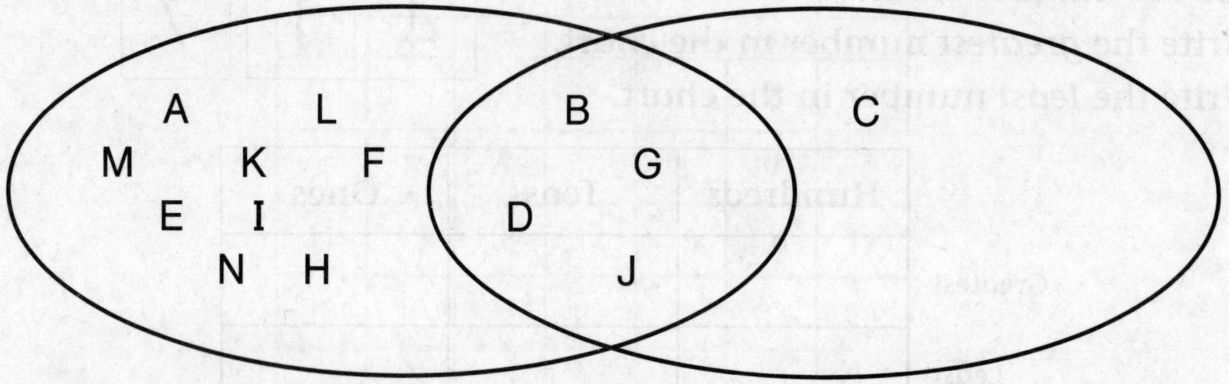

Letters With Lines ONLY **BOTH** **Letters With Curves ONLY**

1. How many letters are made with lines ONLY? ________

2. How many letters are made with curves ONLY? ________

3. How many have lines AND curves? ________

Puzzler

Figure out what a *zerf* is. Then solve.

EACH is a *zerf.*	464	171	323	505
NONE is a *zerf.*	123	77	334	806

Circle all the *zerfs* in the box.

664 949 71 212 828

101 432 818 343

What is the rule for a *zerf*? ________________________________

____

Name ______________________ Date ____________

Number Place

Write the number that is 10 *more*:

364 ______ 635 ______ 711 ______

507 ______ 882 ______ 946 ______

Write the number that is 10 *less*:

135 ______ 592 ______ 867 ______

314 ______ 420 ______ 918 ______

FAST Math

Write how many little boxes in each array.

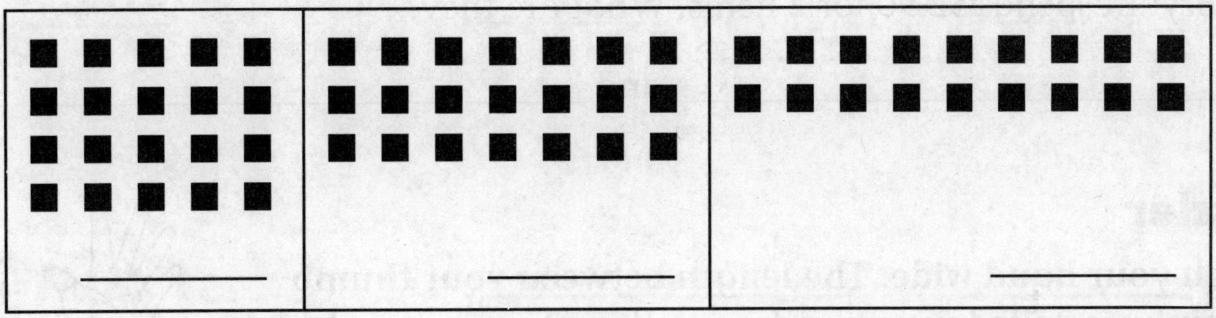

Think Tank

To make 4 pancakes, mix 1 cup pancake mix, 2 eggs, and $\frac{1}{2}$ cup water. How many eggs would you need to make 8 pancakes?

______

Show your work in the tank.

Data Place

Bryant loves bread products! Use the menu to answer the questions.

Breakfast Breads

Item	Price
Bagel With Butter	$1.10
Bagel With Cheese	$1.40
Cinnamon Toast	$ .75
Corn Muffin	$1.20
English Muffin	$ .85
Honey Biscuit	$ .60
Texas Toast	$1.50

1. How much would Bryant spend for 3 honey biscuits?

   ____

2. How much more is a bagel with cheese than a bagel with butter?

   ____

3. Bryant gets an English muffin and cinnamon toast. How much does he spend? __________

4. Bryant spends $2.90 for 2 items. What are they?

   ______________ and ______________

Puzzler

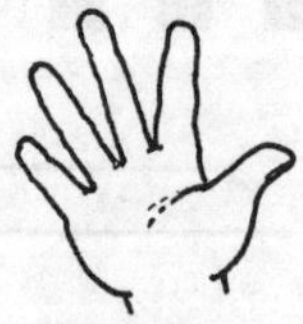

Stretch your hand wide. The length between your thumb and pinky is called your hand *span*. You can use your hand span to estimate and measure. Estimate first. Then measure in spans.

Distance	Estimate Spans	Measure Spans
Across your desk		
Along your arm		
Across an open book		
Height of class door		
Width of a bookshelf		

JUMPSTART 47

Name ____________________ Date ____________

Number Place

Round each number to the nearest hundred.

324 → ______ 567 → ______ 745 → ______ 881 → ______

272 → ______ 481 → ______ 639 → ______ 928 → ______

FAST Math

Add. Look for a pattern.

3 + 3 = ________ 4 + 4 = ________

3 + 3 + 3 = ________ 4 + 4 + 4 = ________

3 + 3 + 3 + 3 = ________ 4 + 4 + 4 + 4 = ________

So, what is five 3s? ________ So, what is five 4s? ________

Think Tank

A flower shop makes spring tulip baskets. Each basket has 6 tulips. How many tulips are in 4 baskets?

There are ________ tulips in 4 baskets.

Show your work in the tank.

Data Place

Trina has $24. Aunt Inez takes her shopping. She lets Trina buy what she wants. The circle graph shows how Trina spent her money.

Use the circle graph to answer the questions.

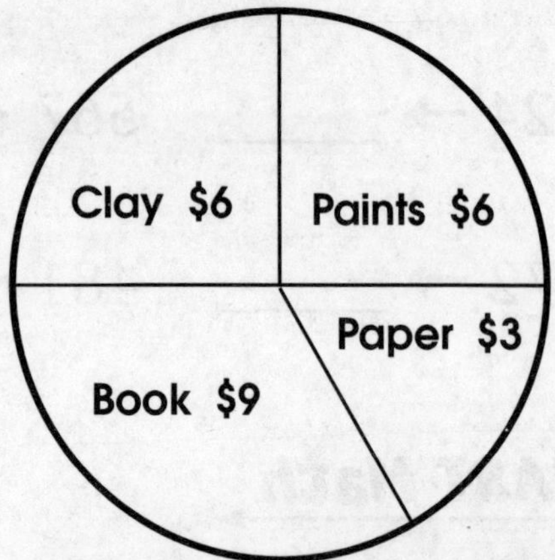

1. How many different kinds of things did Trina buy? __________ How does the circle graph show this? ______________________

____

2. On what did Trina spend $9? ______________

On what did she spend $3? ______________

3. Trina spent the same amount of money on which two kinds of things? ______________________________

Puzzler

X the picture in each row that is different.

1. 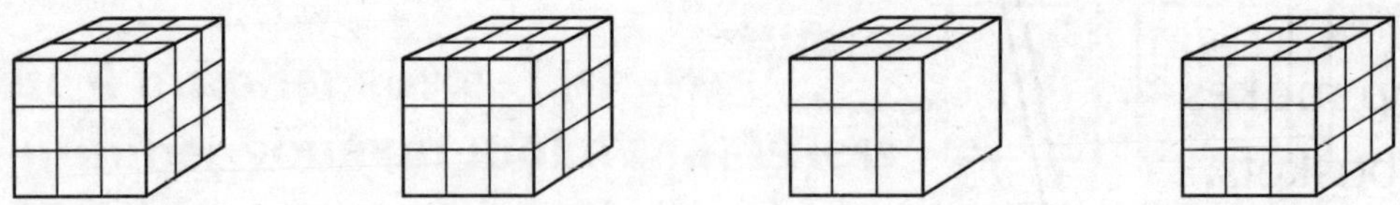

2. 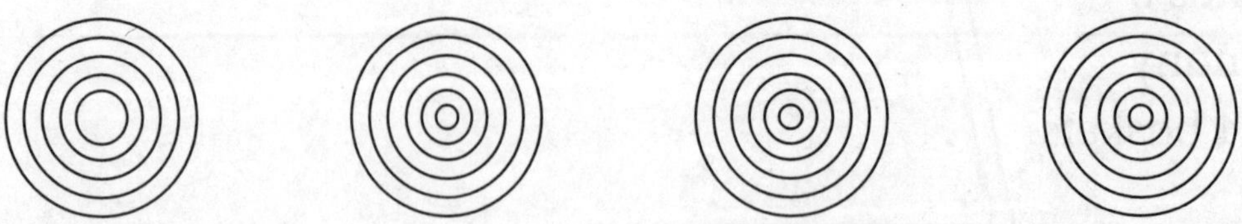

3. 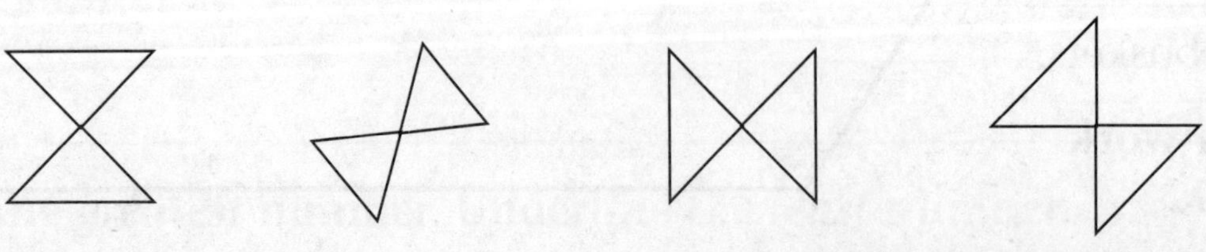

JUMPSTART 48

Name ______________________ Date ______________

Number Place

Count the money. Write how much. Use $ and ¢.

1.		
2.		
3.		

FAST Math

Add. Then find the product.

2 + 2 + 2 + 2 = ______	6 + 6 + 6 = ______
four ______ = ______	three ______ = ______
4×2 = ______	3×6 = ______

Think Tank

A spider has 8 legs. How many legs are there on 3 spiders?

____

Show your work in the tank.

JUMPSTART 48

Side B

Data Place

A table of contents tells what is inside a book. This table of contents is from the book *About Sharks*.

Contents

1	Inside a Shark.	3
2	Where Sharks Live . . .	18
3	Shark Life-Cycle.	29
4	Shark Behavior.	41
5	Sharks and Us.	53
	Index.	62

Use the information to answer the questions.

1. How many chapters are in this book?

   ____

2. What is the title of the first chapter? ________________________

3. What number is the last page in Chapter 3? ________

4. How many pages are in Chapter 5? ________

5. What would you read about on page 45? ____________________

Puzzler

Color squares to make an animal on this grid.

Color squares to make a pattern on this grid.

JUMPSTART 49

Side A

Name ______________________ Date ______________

Number Place

Round each amount to the nearest dollar.

\$1.33 → ________ \$5.79 → ________ \$2.35 → ________

\$3.67 → ________ \$4.28 → ________ \$6.81 → ________

FAST Math

How many groups? Draw a picture to help you.

You have 12 beads. Make groups of 6. How many groups? ______	You have 15 hats. Make groups of 5. How many groups? ______	You have 14 pens. Make groups of 7. How many groups? ______

Think Tank

A game needs teams of 4 children. There are 16 children who want to play. How many teams can be made?

________ teams

Show your work in the tank.

Data Place

Second graders helped plant trees at their school. The table shows what they planted.

Make a pictograph of the data. Write a title. Finish the key. Let △ stand for 2 trees.

Tree	Number Planted
Aspen	8
Empress	12
Poplar	10
Willow	14

____

Key: △ = ________

Puzzler

Pretend that the thick line is a mirror. Half of the design is above it.

Shade the other half below the thick line.

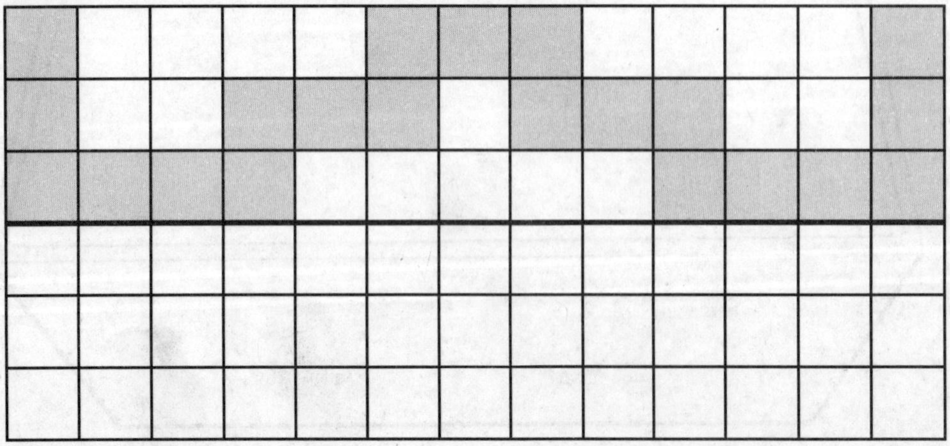

Name ______________________ Date ______________

Number Place

Use the number cards to write:

5	7	3

the greatest 3-digit number __________

the least 3-digit number __________

a number that rounds to 50 __________

a number that rounds to 700 __________

the number nearest to 400 __________

FAST Math

Divide.

16 fish 4 bowls How many fish in each bowl? ______	21 kids 3 teams How many kids on each team? ______	18 plums 6 jars How many plums in each jar? ______

Think Tank

A sports club has 25 players. The coach wants to make 5 equal teams. How many players will be on a team?

____

Show your work in the tank.

JUMPSTART 50

Side B

Data Place

Dad is making a fancy calendar for February. He will use only digits 0–9. He must know how many of each digit to get so he can make all the dates.

Help Dad by tallying each digit below.

FEBRUARY

SUN	MON	TUE	WED	THU	FRI	SAT
1	2	3	4	5	6	7
8	9	10	11	12	13	14
15	16	17	18	19	20	21
22	23	24	25	26	27	28

Digit	Tally
0	
1	
2	
3	
4	

Digit	Tally
5	
6	
7	
8	
9	

Puzzler

Draw the shapes.
Start and stop each line at a dot.

Triangle

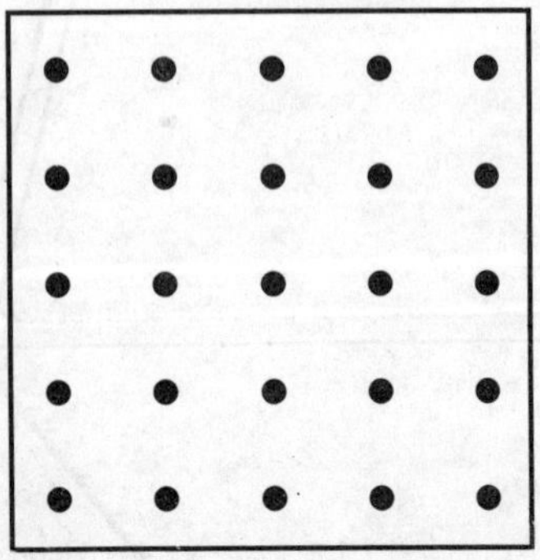

Rectangle

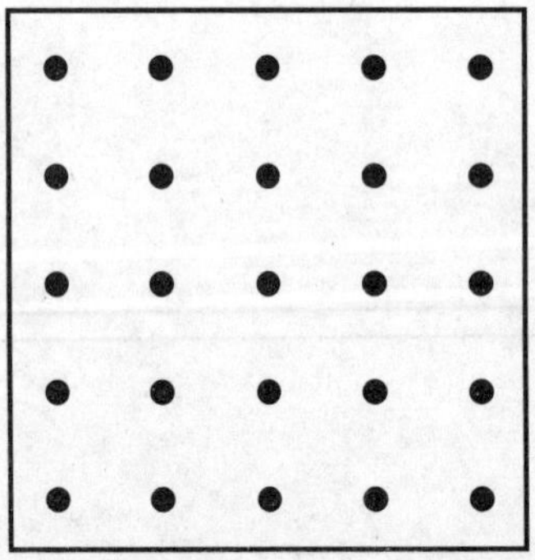

Hexagon

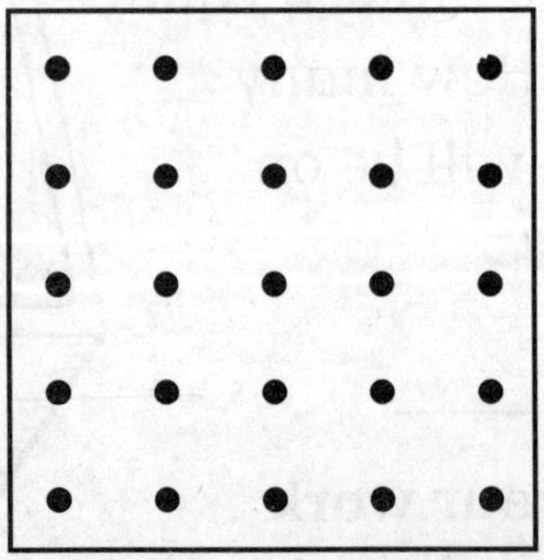

Answers

Jumpstart 1
Number Place: (Top to bottom) 8, 5, 9, 7; 3, 4, 1, 6; 10, 2
Fast Math: (Left to right) 6, 5, 8; 7, 6, 8; 9, 9, 10; answers will vary.
Think Tank: 16
Data Place:

Shape	Tallies
☆	||||
♡	卌 |
◎	卌 |||

1. 8 **2.** 10
Puzzler:

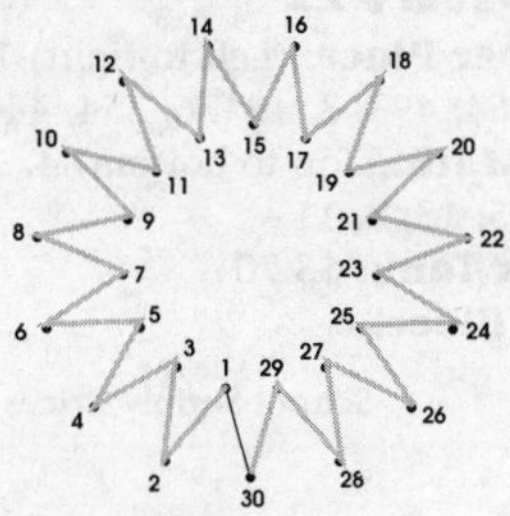

Jumpstart 2
Number Place: Check children's work.
Fast Math: (Left to right) 11, 16, 16; (19), 12, 13; 17, 14, 13
Think Tank: Earth; mostly
Data Place: **1.** 3 **2.** 3 **3.** molly **4.** 2
Puzzler: possible answers—

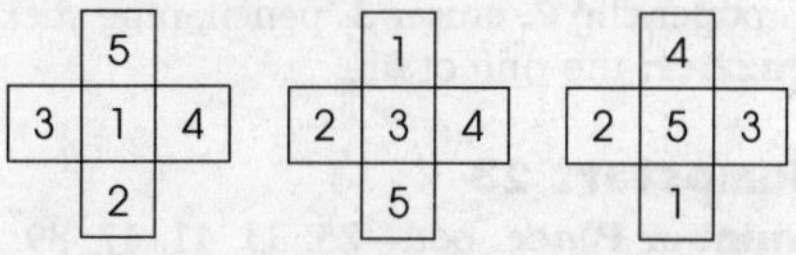

Jumpstart 3
Number Place: 10, 13, 14, 15, 16, 18, 20, 21, 24, 25, 27, 28, 29, 30
Fast Math: 8, 16, 12, 18, 10, 14; 8, 10, 12, 14, 16, 18
Think Tank: 9
Data Place: **1.** eagle **2.** 9 **3.** owl
Puzzler: Check children's pictures.

Jumpstart 4
Number Place:

Fast Math: (Left to right) 14, 13, 16; 15, (19), 18
Think Tank: 48
Data Place: **1.** 4 **2.** heart
Puzzler: **1.** 15 **2.** 19 **3.** 16 **4.** 3 **5.** 2 **6.** 3

Jumpstart 5
Number Place: scramblers
Fast Math: (Left to right) (8), (2), (6); (2), 1, 7; 3, 3, (4)
Think Tank: 4
Data Place: **1.** closet **2.** 5 **3.** closet, chair, bed

Puzzler:

Check children's responses.

Jumpstart 6
Number Place: (Left to right) 37, 49; 78, 81; 54, 100
Fast Math: (Left to right) 6, 8, 8; 10, (9), (9); 6, (7), (5)
Think Tank: 8 adults, 6 children
Data Place: **1.** October **2.** 2 rainy days **3.** 6
Puzzler: Have children demonstrate their solutions.

Jumpstart 7
Number Place: (Left to right) 73, 38, 89; 57, 66, 45
Fast Math: 9, 6, 8, 5, 7, 10; 10, 9, 8, 7, 6, 5
Think Tank: 6
Data Place:

Cousins	Tallies	Number
None	卌 |	6
1 or 2	卌 ||	7
3 or 4	卌 ||||	9
5 or 6	卌	5
7 or 8	||||	4
9 or more	||	2

1. 6 **2.** 9 **3.** 2 **4.** 7 or 8
Puzzler: ostrich

Jumpstart 8
Number Place: (Left to right) 39, 28, 343; 64, 57, 509; 50, 200, 776
Fast Math: 11, 3, 17, 5, 13, (4)
Think Tank: 12 feet
Data Place:

Item	How Many
Forks	XXXX
Glasses	XXXXX
Knives	XXX
Plates	XXXXX
Spoons	X
Key: X = 1 item	

Puzzler: **1.** 8 **2.** 13 **3.** 12 **4.** 11

Jumpstart 9
Number Place: 15, 20, 25, 30, 35, 40, 45, 50, 55, 60, 65, 70, 75, 80, 85, 90, 95
Fast Math: 5 + 8 = 13; 8 + 5 = 13; 13 – 5 = 8; 13 – 8 = 5; 6 + 9 = 15; 9 + 6 = 15; 15 – 9 = 6; 15 – 6 = 9
Think Tank: ● ✖ ● ✖ ; = ☾ ♥ = ☾ ♥ = ; ▲ ◇ ▲ ◇
Data Place: **1.** 27 **2.** Abe found 15 acorns. **3.** Wednesday **4.** Thursday **5.** Monday
Puzzler: (Top to bottom) six, two, one, nine, zero; four, five, seven, three, eight

Jumpstart 10
Number Place: 32, 58, 75
Fast Math: (Top to bottom) 64, 93, 87; 68, 37, 54
Think Tank: $11
Data Place: **1.** peanuts **2.** 15¢ **3.** 44¢ **4.** 60¢ **5.** 85¢ **6.** and **7.** Answers will vary.
Puzzler: **1.** 5 **2.** 9 **3.** 14 **4.** 4 **5.** 10 **6.** 7 **7.** 17 **8.** 3

Jumpstart 11
Number Place: (Left to right) 45, 31, 28; 67, 79, 50
Fast Math: 50, 90, (170), 70, 80, 130
Think Tank: 50¢
Data Place: Answers will vary; check children's work.
Puzzler:

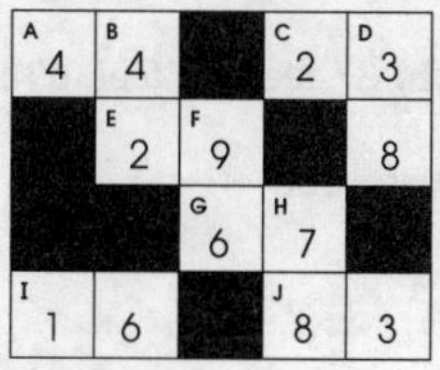

Jumpstart 12
Number Place: (Top to bottom) 30, 53, 99; 41, 18, 36
Fast Math: 2:30 A.M., 7:45 A.M., 1:15 P.M.
Think Tank: Felix
Data Place: **1.** Roberto **2.** Elvis **3.** 2 **4.** Brian, Nina, Wendy
Puzzler: (Top to bottom) hot, jam, pen; ride, quit, chess

Jumpstart 13
Number Place: (Top to bottom) 81, 26, 93; 57, 60, 78, 42
Fast Math:

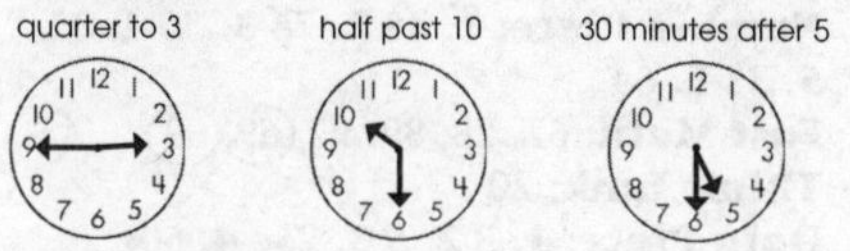

Check children's clock faces.
Think Tank: 67
Data Place:

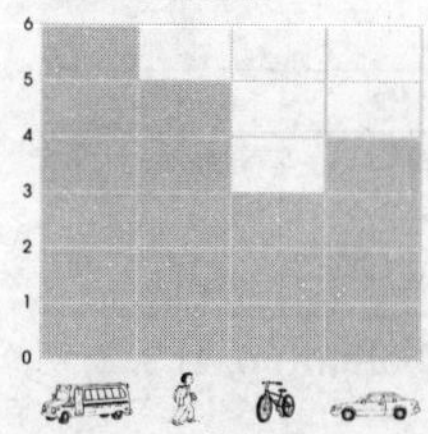

1. 18 **2.** 1 **3.** bus
Puzzler:

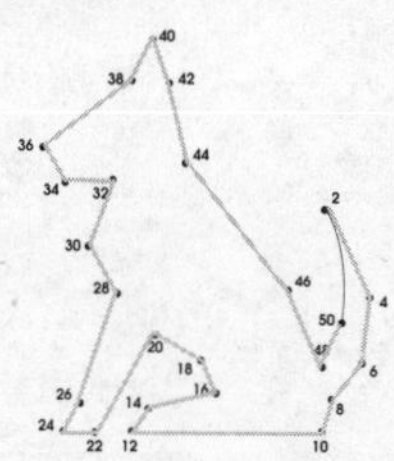

Answers

Jumpstart 14

Number Place: (Top to bottom) 7, 2; 4, 5; 8, 9; 2, 4; 9, 0; 6, 3; 3, 1; 5, 6
Fast Math: Answers may vary, depending on the size of paper clips used. Check children's work.
Think Tank: 29
Data Place:

Sunday	Monday	Tuesday	Wednesday	Thursday	Friday	Saturday
15	16 Paco	17	18 Hari	19 Lia	20	21 Rosa

1. Lia **2.** Paco **3.** Tuesday the 24th
Puzzler: 1. 4 of each coin **2.** 80¢

Jumpstart 15

Number Place: 50 + 6; 40 + 7; 30 + 5; 60 + 0
Fast Math: 37 feet, 22 feet, 69 inches, 20 inches
Think Tank: 100
Data Place:

				Total
2	0	1	2	57¢
2	0	0	**7**	57¢
1	0	6	**2**	57¢
1	**2**	2	**2**	57¢
0	**5**	1	**2**	57¢
0	**4**	**3**	**2**	57¢

Puzzler:

3	4	2	**1**
1	2	**3**	4
2	**1**	4	3
4	3	**1**	**2**

Jumpstart 16

Number Place: 1. 48 **2.** 76 **3.** 50 **4.** 81 **5.** 33 **6.** 64
Fast Math: 67, 78, 89, 97, (69), (69)
Think Tank: 20
Data Place: 1. 3 **2.** 5 **3.** 25¢ **4.** 60¢
Puzzler: 8, 32, 700, ∩IIII, ∩∩∩∩, 𓍢𓍢

Jumpstart 17

Number Place:

22	2 tens 2 ones	2 ✗ 2	twenty-two
53	5 tens 3 ones	50 + 3	thirty-five ✗
✗	4 tens 7 ones	40 + 7	forty-seven
81	1 ten ✗ ones	80 + 1	eighty-one

Fast Math: (Top to bottom) 6, 1; 3, 8; 5, 4; 7, 3; 8, 7
Think Tank: 72
Data Place:

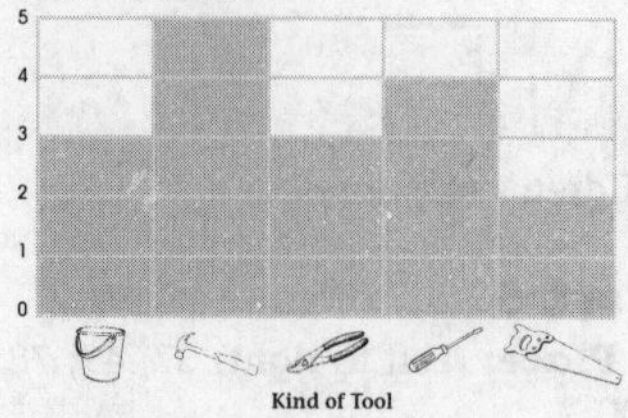

1. 17 **2.** hammers
Puzzler: Answers will vary.

Jumpstart 18

Number Place: 20, 30, 40, 50, 60, 70, 80, 90, 100
Fast Math: 84, 91, 90, 85, 122, (147)
Think Tank: Friday
Data Place: 1. 62°F **2.** Tuesday and Thursday **3.** Friday **4.** Monday
Puzzler:

Jumpstart 19

Number Place: (Left to right) <, >, >; <, >, <
Fast Math: 50, 30, 80; 50, 30, 80; 70, 20, 90
Think Tank: 189
Data Place: 1. (4, 1) **2.** (2, 2) **3.** (3, 4) **4.** (1, 3) **5.** Check children's work.
Puzzler:

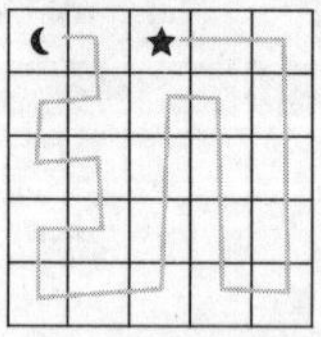

Jumpstart 20

Number Place: 30, 35, 55, 70; 60, 62, 67, 70; 48, 84, 89, 94; 73, 105, 162, 200
Fast Math: 72, 93, (171), 95, 96, 77
Think Tank: $4.79
Data Place: 1. 5 **2.** 15 **3.** 10 **4.** 5 **5.** chocolate **6.** 20
Puzzler:

2	**9**	**4**
7	5	**3**
6	**1**	8

Jumpstart 21

Number Place: 72, 54, 45, 27; 59, 49, 39, 29; 88, 83, 38, 33; 520, 250, 105, 55
Fast Math: 22, 43, (39), 31, 41, 36
Think Tank: 22
Data Place: 1. hot cider **2.** hot cocoa **3.** chicken soup **4.** 53
Puzzler: numbers < 123—7, 12, 45, 99, 106, 112; numbers from 124 to 170—129, 132, 144, 150, 161, 170; numbers > 170—173, 188, 192, 203, 367, 501; check the numbers children add.

Jumpstart 22

Number Place: (Left to right) 16, 45, 87; 218, 364, 493; 3, 49, 76; 354, 440, 702
Fast Math: (Top to bottom) 4, 16; 1, 17; 3, 14; 5, 13; 8, 11
Think Tank: $3.70
Data Place:

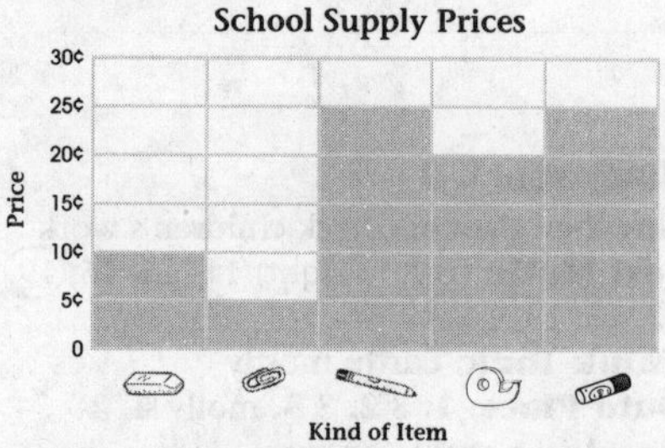

1. paper clip **2.** eraser **3.** pencil, glue stick
Puzzler: the ring of fire

Jumpstart 23

Number Place: odd—25, 33, 41, 47, 89; even—6, 52, 78, 80, 94
Fast Math: 17, 49, 27, 37, (36), 27
Think Tank: 50¢
Data Place:

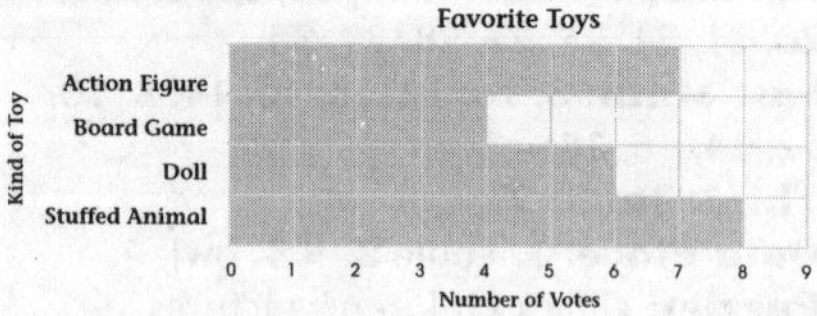

1. stuffed animal
2. action figure and doll
Puzzler: 8, 4, 6, 2

Jumpstart 24

Number Place: (Top to bottom) 6¢, 14¢, 35¢, 40¢; 57¢, 89¢, 90¢, 98¢
Fast Math: 80, 30, 50; 60, 30, 30; 70, 20, 50
Think Tank: 54
Data Place: 1. 5 **2.** 6 **3.** 2
Puzzler: (Left to right) 40, 60, 33, 600, 680, 525

Jumpstart 25
Number Place: (Left to right) 20, 60, 20, 80; 70, 40, 70, 100
Fast Math: 36, 92, 114, 34, 28, 85
Think Tank: 2 quarters and 2 nickels
Data Place:

Butterfly	✔✔✔✔
Crow	✔✔✔✔✔
Rabbit	✔✔✔
Squirrel	✔✔

1. 14 **2.** 9 **3.** 3
Puzzler:

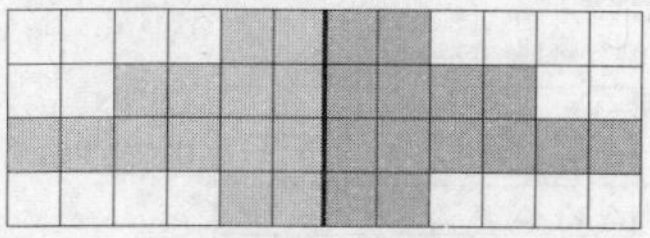

Jumpstart 26
Number Place: (Left to right) 30¢, 40¢, 70¢, 90¢; 30¢, 60¢, 70¢, 80¢
Fast Math: **1.** 89¢ **2.** 72¢ **3.** 66¢
Think Tank: 51
Data Place:

Key	Tally	Number
	𝍸 𝍸	10
	||||	4
	𝍸 ||	7

1. 21 **2.** 6
Puzzler:

15	16	11
10	14	**18**
17	**12**	**13**

Jumpstart 27
Number Place: 20, 21, 22, 23; 39, 40, 41, 42; 68, 69, 70, 71
Fast Math: 70¢, 40¢, 30¢; 70¢, 30¢, 40¢; 90¢, 50¢, 40¢
Think Tank: 200
Data Place: **1.** watch TV, computer **2.** read, art project **3.** 27
Puzzler:

Jumpstart 28
Number Place: 200, 400, 500, 700, 800, 900
Fast Math: $3.93, $1.79, $2.80
Think Tank: 75
Data Place: 7:45, 9:45, 10:15, 11:30
Puzzler: **1.** 12 **2.** 6 **3.** 7

Jumpstart 29
Number Place: (Left to right) 345, 432, 508, 189
Fast Math: $4, $2, $2; $9, $6, $3; $7, $4, $3
Think Tank: cube
Data Place: **1.** (1, 3) **2.** (3, 5) **3.** (5, 1) **4.** (4, 2) **5.** (2, 1)
Puzzler: (Top to bottom) cube, cone, square, circle; sphere, triangle, hexagon, rectangle

Jumpstart 30
Number Place: (Left to right) 487, 914; 896, 502
Fast Math: (Left to right) 900, 700, 900; 500, 600, 700
Think Tank: 100
Data Place: **1.** attic **2.** child's room **3.** dining room
Puzzler: map, boot, ducks, wagon, icicle

Jumpstart 31
Number Place: 5, 4, 2; 7, 8, 5; 3, 6, 9; 8, 0, 4; 2, 1, 7
Fast Math: **1.** 20 centimeters **2.** 3 meters **3.** 12 meters
Think Tank: 12¢
Data Place: **1.** 2 **2.** 6 **3.** 3 **4.** cloudy **5.** Monday, March 8 **6.** It wasn't March yet.
Puzzler:

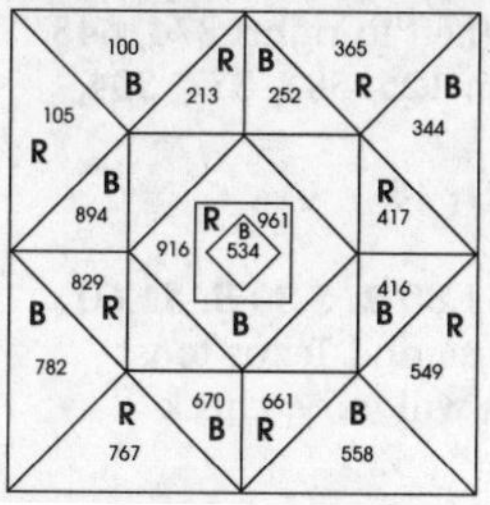

Jumpstart 32
Number Place: 635, 814, 572, 390
Fast Math: 858, 777, 898, 697, 989, 789
Think Tank: 7; check children's drawings.
Data Place: **1.** long cape **2.** $10 **3.** clown wig, magic wand, and witch hat
Puzzler: Answers may vary; check children's work.

Jumpstart 33
Number Place: 700 + 30 + 4; 200 + 90 + 1; 500 + 60 + 8; 400 + 30 + 9
Fast Math: 5, 6; 8, 7; 4, 5; 7, 4
Think Tank: $6
Data Place: **1.** 3 **2.** Layla **3.** Diego **4.** Mason
Puzzler: 443, 463, 483, 473; 852, 752, 742, 762; 781, 771, 791, 691

Jumpstart 34
Number Place: (Top to bottom) 20, 700, 3; 600, 9, 80
Fast Math: 787, 791, 881, 764, 673, 684
Think Tank: 4
Data Place: **1.** Curly, Bleep, Fluff, Snowball **2.** 21 pounds **3.** Fluff and Snowball **4.** He weighs the most.
Puzzler: 3, 2, 7, 9, 6

Jumpstart 35
Number Place: 336, 274, 108, 925, 454, 668
Fast Math: 628, 626, 849, 739, 916, 836
Think Tank: 1:50
Data Place: **1.** Thursday **2.** 30 **3.** November 6 **4.** Sunday
Puzzler: 5; 4

Jumpstart 36
Number Place: (Left to right) 378, 561; 439, 611; 990, 105
Fast Math: 500, 300, 800; 300, 500, 800; 500, 400, 900
Think Tank: May
Data Place: **1.** 37 **2.** summer **3.** winter **4.** fall
Puzzler: **1.** 27 **2.** and **3.** Answers will vary.

Jumpstart 37
Number Place: 159, 160, 161, 162, 163, 165, 166, 167, 168, 170, 171
Fast Math: 795, 757, 929, 849, 658, 989
Think Tank: September 22
Data Place: **1.** 6 **2.** 12 **3.** 2 **4.** sandals, boots
Puzzler: 305, 308, 350, 358, 385, 503, 508, 530, 538, 580

Jumpstart 38
Number Place: 389, 390, 391, 393, 394, 395, 396, 398, 399, 400, 401, 402
Fast Math: 431, 473, 320, 222, 433, 710
Think Tank: sphere; no flat faces
Data Place: **1.** (1, 5) **2.** (2, 4) **3.** (5, 2) **4.** (4, 3) **5.** zebra
Puzzler: circle; 36

Answers

Jumpstart 39

Number Place: 843, 743, 643, 543, 443, 343, 243, 143
Fast Math: 4, 17; 7, 16; 1, 15; 3, 13; 8, 10
Think Tank: 599
Data Place:

Books	Tally	Number
None	II	2
1 to 5	𝍸 I	6
6-10	𝍸 𝍸 II	12
11-15	𝍸 𝍸 𝍸	15
16 or more	𝍸 III	8

1. 2 **2.** 12 **3.** 8
Puzzler: 19, 65, 90

Jumpstart 40

Number Place: (Left to right) 347, 481, 798; 809, 532, 960
Fast Math: 547; 227, (428) 233, (336) 107
Think Tank: 10; 5
Data Place: The difference between most and least jumps is 25.

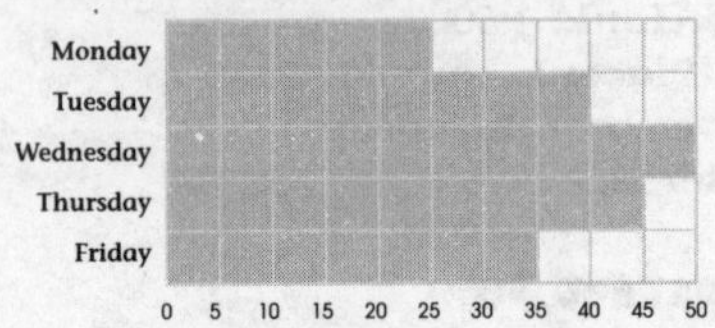

Puzzler: Check children's coloring.

Jumpstart 41

Number Place: (Left to right) 733, 138, 908; 527, 646, 459
Fast Math: 270, (473) 354, 450, (291) 282
Think Tank: 213
Data Place: **1.** 187 **2.** 351 **3.** Friday **4.** 30
Puzzler: 2 coins—6¢, 11¢, 26¢, 15¢, 30¢, 35¢; 3 coins—16¢, 31¢, 36¢, 40¢

Jumpstart 42

Number Place: (Left to right) 246, 273, 148; 624, 565, 809; 480, 800, 967
Fast Math: (37) 138, 83, 983, 255, 790
Think Tank: **1.** 50¢ **2.** 55¢
Data Place: **1.** 5, 10, 15, 20, 25, 30 **2.** 2, 4, 6, 8, 10, 12, 14, 16, 18, 20, 22, 24, 26, 28, 30 **3.** fives only: 5, 15, 25; twos only: 2, 4, 6, 8, 12, 14, 16, 18, 22, 24, 26, 28; both: 10, 20, 30
Puzzler:

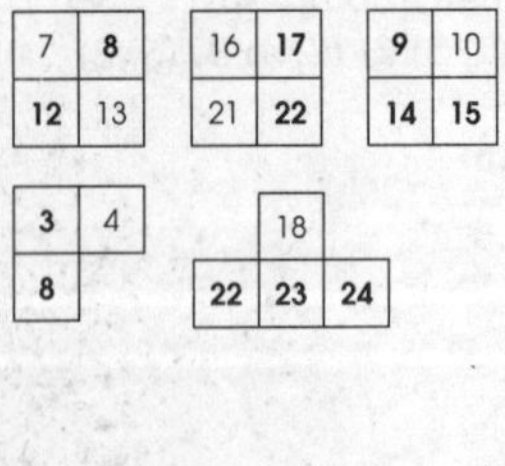

Jumpstart 43

Number Place: (Left to right) <, >, <; >, >, <
Fast Math: \$3.44, \$5.59, \$2.54, \$9.38, (\$3.50)
Think Tank: 400
Data Place: **1.** 30 **2.** camel **3.** bear and horse **4.** 40
Puzzler: **1.** I **2.** U **3.** A **4.** E **5.** O **6.** Y

Jumpstart 44

Number Place: 354, 405, 530, 545; 814, 819, 914, 948; 728, 783, 857, 875; 460, 462, 467, 470
Fast Math: Check children's shadings.
Think Tank: 26, 32; 65, 76
Data Place:

Vowel	Tally	Number
a	III	3
e	𝍸	5
i	II	2
o	II	2
u	II	2

14 vowels in all

Puzzler: 1621, 1901, 1929, 1957

Jumpstart 45

Number Place: greatest—741; least—147
Fast Math: $\frac{1}{4}, \frac{1}{3}, \frac{1}{2}, \frac{1}{6}$
Think Tank: \$5.25
Data Place: lines only—T, V, W, X, Y, Z; curves only—O, S, U; both—P, Q, R **1.** 15 **2.** 7 **3.** 4
Puzzler: *zerfs:* 949, 212, 101, 828, 818, 343; 3-digit palindrome number

Jumpstart 46

Number Place: (Left to right) 374, 645, 721; 517, 892, 956; 125, 582, 857; 304, 410, 908
Fast Math: 20, 21, 18
Think Tank: 4
Data Place: **1.** \$1.80 **2.** \$.30 **3.** \$1.60 **4.** bagel with cheese and Texas toast
Puzzler: Answers will vary; check children's work.

Jumpstart 47

Number Place: (Left to right) 300, 600, 700, 900; 300, 500, 600, 900
Fast Math: 6, 9, 12, 15; 8, 12, 16, 20
Think Tank: 24
Data Place: **1.** 4; it has four sections. **2.** book; paper **3.** clay and paints
Puzzler: **1.** 3rd figure **2.** 1st figure **3.** 2nd figure

Jumpstart 48

Number Place: **1.** \$1.63 **2.** \$3.52 **3.** \$2.80
Fast Math: 8, 2s, 8, 8; 18, 6s, 18, 18
Think Tank: 24
Data Place: **1.** 5 **2.** Inside a Shark **3.** 40 **4.** 9 **5.** shark behavior
Puzzler: Check children's drawings.

Jumpstart 49

Number Place: (Left to right) \$1, \$6, \$2; \$4, \$4, \$7
Fast Math: 2, 3, 2
Think Tank: 4
Data Place:

Different Trees at School

Aspen	△ △ △ △
Empress	△ △ △ △ △ △
Poplar	△ △ △ △ △
Willow	△ △ △ △ △ △ △

Key: △ = 2 trees

Titles may vary.

Puzzler:

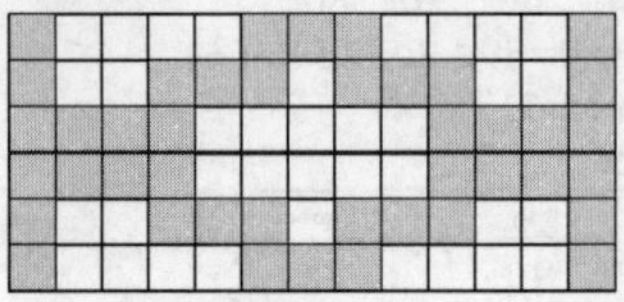

Jumpstart 50

Number Place: 753, 357, 53, 735, 375
Fast Math: 4, 7, 3
Think Tank: 5
Data Place:

Digit	Tally
0	II
1	𝍸 𝍸 III
2	𝍸 𝍸 II
3	III
4	III

Digit	Tally
5	III
6	III
7	III
8	III
9	II

Puzzler: Shapes may vary; check children's drawings.